WHY FEW ARE CHOSEN

Dag Heward-Mills

Parchment House

Unless otherwise stated, all Scripture quotations are taken from the King James Version of the Bible.

WHY FEW ARE CHOSEN

First published 2022 by Parchment House

Find out more about Dag Heward-Mills at:

Healing Jesus Campaign
Email: evangelist@daghewardmills.org
Website: www.daghewardmills.org
Facebook: Dag Heward-Mills
Twitter: @EvangelistDag

ISBN : 978-1-64330-613-1

Contents

CHAPTER 1

Many Are Called but Few Are Chosen

For many are called, but few are chosen.

Matthew 22:14

All through the Bible we see a pattern of many people being called but few being chosen in the end. This book is about how this pattern of many people being called and few being chosen comes about.

It is a fact of life that many are offered opportunities but few end up making the most of these opportunities. Many start out in primary school. Many go to secondary school. But few are able to go to the university.

Many people have a first degree but few have PhDs. There are many factors that cause the initial group to whittle down to such small numbers.

All through the word of God, we see many people being called to God. The word "come" appears over two thousand, one hundred and six times in the Bible. God is an invitational God. He is always inviting, drawing and calling people.

God so loved the whole world that He gave His only Son to save the world. Unfortunately, the whole world is not coming to Christ. Very few have responded to this great offer of salvation through Jesus Christ.

Come unto me all ye that labour and are heavy laden and I will give you rest (Matthew 11:28). Obviously, the whole world is heavily laden with sin. But the whole world is not coming to Jesus Christ.

God wants many people to work for Him! Many are called to the ministry but many do not respond. In the end very few people become ministers of the gospel.

In this book, you will see that there are many invitees, many servants, many virgins, many seeds, many Israelites and many spies that are offered a chance to work. I feel sad to report that few end up being chosen!

Through this book, you will work hard to become one of the few who are chosen.

You will escape whatever evil causes people not to be chosen!

CHAPTER 2

Few Are Chosen because They Make Light of Their Calling

And Jesus answered and spake unto them again by parables, and said, The kingdom of heaven is like unto a certain king, which made a marriage for his son, And sent forth his servants to call them that were bidden to the wedding: and they would not come. Again, he sent forth other servants, saying, Tell them which are bidden, Behold, I have prepared my dinner: my oxen and my fatlings are killed, and all things are ready: come unto the marriage.

BUT THEY MADE LIGHT OF IT, AND WENT THEIR WAYS, ONE TO HIS FARM, ANOTHER TO HIS MERCHANDISE: And the remnant took his servants, and entreated them spitefully, and slew them. But when the king heard thereof, he was wroth: and he sent forth his armies, and destroyed those murderers, and burned up their city. Then saith he to his servants, The wedding is ready, but they which were bidden were not worthy. Go ye therefore into the highways, and as many as ye shall find, bid to the marriage. So those servants went out into the highways, and gathered together all as many as they found, both bad and good: and the wedding was furnished with guests. And when the king came in to see the guests, he saw there a man which had not on a wedding garment: And he saith unto him, Friend, how camest thou in hither not having a wedding garment? And he was speechless. Then said the king to the servants, Bind him hand and foot, and take him away, and cast him into outer darkness; there shall be weeping and gnashing of teeth. FOR MANY ARE CALLED, BUT FEW ARE CHOSEN.

Matthew 22:1-14

Be careful you do not make light of the call of God. Do not trivialise the call you are getting from the Lord. I know many people who work in the secular world but should actually work in the church. They are priests who shunned their calling and went after secular things.

Many curses are released because people make light of God's calling.

I remember a story I heard from Derek Prince, the great teacher of the Word. He spoke about how the Viceroy (the British Governor of India) invited one of the commanders of the British Army in India for dinner. This army commander decided not to go because he was busy or did not feel disposed to go. When the Viceroy realised that the officer did not honour the invitation, it sparked a big problem for the officer. Of course, the Viceroy felt slighted by the absence of this invited officer. I think the officer was relieved of his command or sacked for not honouring the invitation for dinner. Indeed, God has also invited us for a great dinner. If spurning an invitation of the Viceroy could lead to such trouble, then how much more trouble can we expect for refusing the invitation and call of God? So why do people make light of the call?

1. **People make light of the call because they do not know that they will get into trouble for rejecting the call of God.**

   Now the word of the LORD came unto Jonah the son of Amittai, saying, arise, go to Nineveh, that great city, and cry against it; for their wickedness is come up before me. But Jonah rose up to flee unto Tarshish from the presence of the LORD, and went down to Joppa; and he found a ship going to Tarshish: so he paid the fare thereof, and went down into it, to go with them unto Tarshish from the presence of the LORD. BUT THE LORD SENT OUT A GREAT WIND INTO

THE SEA, AND THERE WAS A MIGHTY TEMPEST IN THE SEA, SO THAT THE SHIP WAS LIKE TO BE BROKEN.

Jonah 1:1-4

Go and ask Jonah what happened to him when he made light of the call of God and went about his own business. Jonah met storm after storm and trouble after trouble.

Jonah encountered an incredible storm and then encountered an angry mob who voted to throw him into the raging sea. Jonah then was attacked and swallowed by a large fish. For three days and nights Jonah was in the belly of the whale and in the midst of great difficulty. Trouble awaits those who make light of the call of God.

2. People make light of their calling because they do not find the call of God attractive.

God calls many people! The world also calls people. The world offers people great jobs and opportunities. After university, people are offered all kinds of amazing opportunities. They are given a chance to travel all over the world and to work in glassy high-rise buildings.

When God's call comes, it looks so drab and dreary. Come and work in the church! Go to the mission field! Go to this poor country! Leave your home! Leave your amazing secular job and do not seek greater incomes and money.

This is why many people make light the call of God.

3. People make light of their calling by esteeming secular things more highly than they should.

When I was in the university, there were other people who felt they were called by God. I remember a friend who said he was called to be a teacher of the Word. One night I prayed with him under some tall trees in a garden. He described how God had called him to teach the Word. I also spoke about my calling and how I also wanted to be a teacher of the Word. I told him that I had a dream that one day I would sit on a mountain and many people would come to me on that mountain, and I would teach them the word of God. We all felt the call of God. However, after school, he made light of the calling and today he is not in the ministry at all. The last I heard of him, he was not in the ministry.

How did this person make light of his calling? How do people make light of their calling? You make light of your calling when you take your secular opportunities more seriously than your call to ministry. Most people do not intend to make light of their calling. People do not intend to abandon their ministries. But in the end that is what happens.

4.   **People make light of their calling by postponing their responses to God.**

Jesus saith unto them, my meat is to do the will of him that sent me, and to finish his work. Say not ye, There are yet four months, and then cometh harvest? Behold, I say unto you, lift up your eyes, and look on the fields; for they are white already to harvest.

John 4:34-35

Few are chosen because they make light of their calling. The call of God is postponed indefinitely and ends up never happening. Anything you can postpone is not that urgent or important.

It can wait! It's just the call of God! Jesus said do not say there is time for the harvest. Do not postpone your ministry for even four months.

CHAPTER 3

Few Are Chosen because They Treat God's Servants Spitefully

The kingdom of heaven is like unto a certain king, which made a marriage for his son, And sent forth his servants to call them that were bidden to the wedding: and they would not come. Again, he sent forth other servants, saying, tell them which are bidden, Behold, I have prepared my dinner: my oxen and my fatlings are killed, and all things are ready: come unto the marriage. But they made light of it, and went their ways, one to his farm, another to his merchandise: AND THE REMNANT TOOK HIS SERVANTS, AND ENTREATED THEM SPITEFULLY, AND SLEW THEM.

Matthew 22:2-6

Criticizing anointed men is one way of treating God's servants spitefully. Many are called to serve the Lord. Unfortunately, many people make the mistake of treating God's servants spitefully. You do not have to go far to hear someone making fun of a pastor. You do not have to live very long before you hear someone saying nasty things about men of God.

There is always someone ready to speak against God's anointed servants. It is easy to be pulled into criticizing God's servants and treating them spitefully. Once you speak against a servant of God, it is not likely that you will be used much by the Lord.

You do not attract that which you attack! Anything you attack will run away from you. If you attack the anointing, it will go far away from you.

You cannot learn from someone whom you hate. You can only learn from someone you admire. You will not receive power, healing and blessings from something you despise.

One day, Kenneth Hagin described how he went to his auntie's house. His auntie was very ill and near death. This auntie had always criticized pastors and had no faith in the ministers of God. She used to say, "They are all fake. They are just in it for the money." By the time of this visit, this old lady had been bedridden and hardly ever moved from the position in which she lay. She was told that Kenneth Hagin was around. They tried to remind her, "Remember your nephew who became a preacher? Do you remember Ken, the one who was made a preacher?" She nodded her head. She wanted to see him! Remember she was dying.

When Kenneth Hagin was brought in to see her, she stirred in the bed. She beckoned to him. Kenneth Hagin bent over her.

He said her eyes were like glass marbles.

She said, "Ken! Ken!"

He responded to the old dying lady.

Then she said, "Ken, tell me there's no God.

"Ken, tell me there's no hell."

"Ken, tell me there's no heaven."

"Ken, tell me there's no eternity."

But he couldn't! He couldn't say there was no hell because there is a hell.

She could not receive from him.

He heard her voice coming from deep within her throat, "Tell me there's no heaven."

She couldn't even be saved through this great prophet in her last moments on earth.

You cannot receive anything from people you treat spitefully

This is why few are chosen, because they treat God's servants spitefully. When you treat God's servants spitefully, you cannot receive anything from them. You will never progress into ministry and never flow in the anointing because of the strikes you have made against God's servants.

CHAPTER 4

Few Are Chosen because They Are Not Dressed Properly

And when the king came in to see the guests, he saw there a man which had not on a wedding garment: And he saith unto him, FRIEND, HOW CAMEST THOU IN HITHER NOT HAVING A WEDDING GARMENT? And he was speechless. Then said the king to the servants, Bind him hand and foot, and take him away, and cast him into outer darkness; there shall be weeping and gnashing of teeth. For many are called, but few are chosen.

Matthew 22:11-14

The man who was rejected from the wedding was not dressed properly. When you are invited to a programme, you are expected to dress properly and show respect for the invitation.

Respect the call of God and you will be chosen. How do you respect the call? How do you respect an invitation? By dressing properly and showing up with your best behaviour!

If you respect an invitation to a wedding, you will dress properly. If you do not think much of the invitation, you will come shabbily dressed. You cannot dress anyhow for a wedding. The master of the house was displeased because this man had come without respecting the invitation.

After hearing the call of God, it is important that you dress properly. What does the dressing properly mean?

In the Bible, your dressing often speaks of holiness. The white robes depict the holiness of the saints. God expects those who are called, to dress properly.

You will be judged because you did not dress properly in response to the call of God.

God is not pleased with fornicators, adulterers and sexual perverts. He wants to have pure and holy priests to stand before Him all day; and all night. It is time for you to pay the price to carry the anointing of God.

I remember a hotel in which I once stayed that did not allow people to walk around in certain clothes. You were not allowed to come to the lobby in your swimsuit, or your towel or your slippers. Why is that? People who dressed that way would degrade the hotel. The hotel wanted to keep a dignified image in its lobby. In the same way, you cannot simply wear anything in the house of the Lord.

On another occasion, I visited a golf course. I saw so many rules on what you were allowed to wear. Even on the golf course, we were not allowed to just dress anyhow. If a golf course and a hotel can require you to dress in a certain way, how much more the house of the Lord? It is time for you to pay the price and dress properly.

What do you have to get rid of in order to live a pure life? Is it a man? Is it a woman? Is it a friend who is preventing you from being pure? I can tell you in advance that there is no human being who is worth giving up your call for. It is just a matter of time before that person will be tired of you and wish that he had never met you.

Rise up and pay the price to get the right clothes so that you can attend the banquet with the few that are chosen. Indeed, many are called but few are chosen because people are not prepared to pay the price to serve the Lord.

CHAPTER 5

Few Are Chosen because They Are Offended and Become Devils

This is that bread which came down from heaven: not as your fathers did eat manna, and are dead: he that eateth of this bread shall live for ever. These things said he in the synagogue, as he taught in Capernaum. Many therefore of his disciples, when they had heard this, said, this is an hard saying; who can hear it? When Jesus knew in himself that his disciples murmured at it, he said unto them, DOTH THIS OFFEND YOU? What and if ye shall see the Son of man ascend up where he was before? ... But there are some of you that believe not. For Jesus knew from the beginning who they were that believed not, and who should betray him. And he said, Therefore said I unto you, that no man can come unto me, except it were given unto him of my Father. FROM THAT TIME MANY OF HIS DISCIPLES WENT BACK, AND WALKED NO MORE WITH HIM.

John 6:58-62,64-66

Then said Jesus unto the twelve, Will ye also go away? Then Simon Peter answered him, Lord, to whom shall we go? thou hast the words of eternal life. And we believe and are sure that thou art that Christ, the Son of the living God. Jesus answered them, HAVE NOT I CHOSEN YOU TWELVE, AND ONE OF YOU IS A DEVIL? He spake of Judas Iscariot the son of Simon: for he it was that should betray him, being one of the twelve.

John 6:67-71

Getting offended is one of the commonest things that can happen to you in the course of your ministry. On the scale of evil, human beings are just next to devils. There is so much evil in a human being! Everybody feels that the other person is the epitome of evil. Everyone sings this song: "He is jealous of me!" "She is angry with me!" "They don't like me!" "They want to take my position!" "They are lying to me!" "They hate me!"

These are the commonest things that human beings say about each other.

Everyone says the other person is evil. We keep on offending each other and hurts keep on building up.

Jesus knew that His disciples would be offended. The Bible says that most of His disciples left Him and would walk no more with Him. Jesus asked His other disciples whether they would also leave. Jesus said to them, "If this offends you, I do not know what you are going to do in the future." From that time, many of His disciples went back. They walked no longer with Him. They were offended at this message.

There are many things that will offend you as you serve the Lord. Many are called but many are also offended! What can offend you? I could list many things that have offended me throughout my ministry. One day, I heard a piece of advice from a senior minister. He said, "Always keep your heart pure and free of hurts." As the years have gone by, I have realized how important his advice was.

There are many things that can prick you and hurt you. When you meet an Absalom, you will have a reason to be hurt. I once had sons and daughters whom I loved dearly in the ministry. These sons and daughters hurt me greatly. I could not believe my eyes and my ears when I thought of what these people had done to me. People who specialized in throwing knives at me in return for my love. That was an unfortunate experience! But I had to get used to it and forgive them. Such is the experience with an Absalom; someone who hurts his father! Forgiveness is the reason why you still have people in your life after many years. If you allow offence to drive you out, you will be out forever. If Jesus had followed the hurts that He experienced at the cross, He would not have had anybody to send to the world. The people He had sent to the world to preach the gospel denied Him and said they did not know Him or they had not seen Him before. Meanwhile He had spent three years with them, having dinners, lunches and many good times with them.

They said they had heard of Him in the news but they had not had any personal encounters with Him. Then they asked to be excused; and they vanished into the night. What friends indeed they were! A friend in need is a friend indeed! When you are in need and you have no friend, then you truly have no friend.

As you go along in the ministry, you are going to meet Judas Iscariot. Judas is someone you treasure! Judas is someone you care for! Judas is someone you favour! Judas is someone you elevate above others! Judas is someone who is given more money than the others! Judas is someone whose faults are overlooked! Judas is someone who has two loyalties; he loves the Lord but he has other contacts outside! Judas is part of the innermost circle. You cannot be a Judas unless you are very close to the top. You must be as close as skin to qualify to be a Judas.

Judas offered his outside contacts information. He said, "I know Him very well. I can help you." Perhaps, Judas did not even realise when his loyalties switched from Jesus to the Pharisees. He must have maintained friendships with the Pharisees for so many years.

With the offer of a little money to help Judas get rich quickly, Judas entered the darkest chapter of the history of mankind, by becoming the one to betray the Son of God. Indeed, when Jesus was captured, Jesus had no comment to make to Judas. He was hurt! He was broken! I think that is why He did not say anything to Judas. Better not to comment! As they led Jesus away to the cross, Jesus could not help thinking about Judas; "How I loved this young man! I helped him! I paid his school fees! I loved him. I appointed him and I brought him close. I even made him my treasurer, when there were other more qualified people like James and John."

Jesus went to the cross thinking of the purposes of God and not the treachery of Judas Iscariot. After Jesus rose from the dead, He never mentioned Judas even once.

Judas is a bad experience that many ministers will have. You must learn to overcome the pain and the hurt ministered to you by those you trust. Jesus would not be deterred by His offences and hurts.

He called His disciples together for a lunch in Galilee. Three times Jesus asked Peter, "Do you love me?" (John 21:15-17). He asked him because He was not really sure of Peter's love any more. People who love you do not deny you. People who love you do not keep silent when you are in trouble! People who love you remember the times you had together!

Dear friend, do not let offences turn you away from your mission. Jesus Christ was not turned away from His mission by the hurts and offences of ministry. Many are called but few are chosen! Many are offended and simply cannot carry on in the ministry. Keep moving! Keep pressing on! There is more ahead! You must learn to forgive because you have been forgiven a lot.

CHAPTER 6

Few Are Chosen because They Are Not Obedient in Little Things

For the kingdom of heaven is as a man travelling into a far country, who called his own servants, and delivered unto them his goods. And unto one he gave five talents, to another two, and to another one; to every man according to his several ability; and straightway took his journey. Then he that had received the five talents went and traded with the same, and made them other five talents. And likewise he that had received two, he also gained other two. BUT HE THAT HAD RECEIVED ONE WENT AND DIGGED IN THE EARTH, AND HID HIS LORD'S MONEY.

Matthew 25:14-18

Few are chosen because they are not obedient in small things. The storms of missions, the storms of leadership, the storms of marriage are coming to all missionaries. Without obedience in the little things there is no hope that you will do well!

Many are called and few are chosen because they do not obey God in little things. My experience in ministry is that many little things make up the great ministry that God has called you to.

The reason why it is difficult to follow a man of God is because he is doing many little things. Those little things are working together for his good. I remember listening to Derek Prince one night. He spoke about how God had called him. He spoke about a strong warning that the Lord had given him when He commissioned him into the ministry. He said the Lord told him, "You must obey me in the big things and you must also obey me in the little things."

I have sent out many missionaries myself. I have found that those who do well are those who obey me in the little things. One day I sat with a missionary. We discussed his church. I realised he was concerned about many big things. He was concerned about prayer, fasting and achieving church growth in many different ways. But I had two simple instructions for him. These instructions looked like little things but they were the main instructions. This missionary did not obey me because the instructions seemed frivolous.

A year later, this missionary was a failure! After eight years he had still not broken through in ministry. I still gave him the same instructions I had given him eight years earlier. He simply had not learned the lesson of obeying in little things.

If you take an airline, you will find out that the differences between airlines are not big things. They are little things! The big things are the same! The makers of the plane are the same! There are only two major plane manufacturers; Airbus and Boeing. There are not many variations in the types of aircrafts.

An aircraft will either be a Boeing plane or an Airbus. It is the little things in the plane that matter. The service, the attendants, the pleasantness of the staff and whether they are on time. Those are the things that make an airline successful.

Today, it is important that you believe that little things make a difference. One day, I was talking to a couple that was getting married. I told them something that would be very good for them to do. I knew that the advice that I gave them sounded like a little thing. But it was the main thing! It was the most important thing for their marriage. I guess it was not one of the big topics they had been taken through during their marriage counselling sessions.

When the couple heeded my advice, they had the happiest times of their lives. Indeed, they kept coming back to tell me the happy times they were having together. What difference obedience in little things makes to a person's life!

Over the years, I have been convinced that obeying God in little things is as important as obeying God in big things.

In the story that Jesus told, the man refused to use his one talent because it was too little. It is important that you obey God in the little things. It is going to make a big difference in your life and ministry. Amen!

CHAPTER 7

Few Virgins Are Chosen Because of Foolishness

Then shall the kingdom of heaven be likened unto ten virgins, which took their lamps, and went forth to meet the bridegroom. And five of them were wise, AND FIVE WERE FOOLISH. They that were foolish took their lamps, and took no oil with them: But the wise took oil in their vessels with their lamps. While the bridegroom tarried, they all slumbered and slept. And at midnight there was a cry made, behold, the bridegroom cometh; go ye out to meet him.

Then all those virgins arose, and trimmed their lamps. AND THE FOOLISH SAID UNTO THE WISE, GIVE US OF YOUR OIL; FOR OUR LAMPS ARE GONE OUT. BUT THE WISE ANSWERED, SAYING, NOT SO; LEST THERE BE NOT ENOUGH FOR US AND YOU: BUT GO YE RATHER TO THEM THAT SELL, AND BUY FOR YOURSELVES.

And while they went to buy, the bridegroom came; and they that were ready went in with him to the marriage: and the door was shut. Afterward came also the other virgins, saying, Lord, Lord, open to us. But he answered and said, Verily I say unto you, I know you not. Watch therefore, for ye know neither the day nor the hour wherein the Son of man cometh.

Matthew 25:1-13

Many are called but few are chosen! For various reasons, few end up being chosen! In this story, we see ten virgins being invited to a wedding. Few ended up being chosen to actually participate in the wedding.

Foolishness is revealed when a person is short-sighted and cannot see the future. A foolish person cannot see the storm on the horizon. He carries on as though there is no problem.

A wise man will build a house on a rock because he knows that a storm will come. What will happen when the storm arrives? Will your house be standing after the storm has passed? Are you wise or foolish?

Why were some virgins described as foolish? Someone who sits in an exam room totally unprepared for the exam that is set before him can only be described as a fool. It is time to prepare for the future. It is time to be one of the wise virgins. Do not be left out by being a foolish virgin!

Three Ways to Overcome Foolishness

1. Overcome foolishness by expecting to suffer for a long time.

   So then, since Christ suffered physical pain, you must ARM YOURSELVES WITH THE SAME ATTITUDE HE HAD, AND BE READY TO SUFFER, TOO. For if you have suffered physically for Christ, you have finished with sin. You won't spend the rest of your lives chasing your own desires, but you will be anxious to do the will of God.

   1 Peter 4:1-2 (NLT)

   Prepare your mind to suffer for a long time. Five of the virgins were not expecting to go through that length of suffering. Ministry involves a long period of suffering. There is nothing like ministry without suffering. People drop off when they go through hard times. You must arm yourself with the mind that you are going to suffer for a long time. If you do not arm yourself with a certain mind, you will be discouraged by what you go through. You should not expect to have a big church, a big car or a big house anytime soon. You should expect to be in difficulty for a long time. It is only when you arm yourself with this kind of mind that you will overcome foolishness.

2.   Overcome foolishness by preparing for a long war.

> **Joshua made war a long time with all those kings.**
>
> **Joshua 11:18**

> **When thou shalt besiege a city a long time, in making war against it to take it, thou shalt not destroy the trees thereof by forcing an axe against them: for thou mayest eat of them, and thou shalt not cut them down (for the tree of the field is man's life) to employ them in the siege:**
>
> **Deuteronomy 20:19**

> **Now there was long war between the house of Saul and the house of David: but David waxed stronger and stronger, and the house of Saul waxed weaker and weaker.**
>
> **2 Samuel 3:1**

Many wars last a long time. Joshua fought for a long time. Many cities have to be besieged for a long time before they surrender.

Many conflicts last for a long time! Ministry is war! You should expect to be fighting all your life. There is going to be a long war between you and the devil. Satan is not going to give up easily. He is going to try different methods to take you on and to destroy you.

We long for peace and calm but unfortunately, there is going to be a long war between you and the enemy.

Satan will not leave you alone. He will seek to destroy you time and time again. At the end of your life, you will probably come to the conclusion that problems do not go away. They just get modified! You will also come to the conclusion that conflicts do not easily end.

3. Overcome foolishness by preparing for long delays.

The Lord is not slack concerning his promise, as some men count slackness; but is longsuffering to us-ward, not willing that any should perish, but that all should come to repentance.

2 Peter 3:9

There can be long delays in the ministry! There are changes we all expect to happen immediately. You expect growth immediately! You expect people to be transformed immediately. You expect your husband to change immediately. You expect your wife to change immediately. You expect the seed that you have sown to germinate immediately. You are going to discover that there are long delays in the ministry.

CHAPTER 8

Few Virgins Are Chosen because They Do Not Have Enough of Something

And at midnight there was a cry made, Behold, the bridegroom cometh; go ye out to meet him. Then all those virgins arose, and trimmed their lamps. And the foolish said unto the wise, give us of your oil; for our lamps are gone out. But the wise answered, saying, not so; lest THERE BE NOT ENOUGH FOR US and you: but go ye rather to them that sell, and buy for yourselves.

Matthew 25:6-9

Many are called but few are chosen! For various reasons, few end up being chosen! In this story, we see ten virgins being invited to a wedding. Few ended up being chosen to actually participate in the wedding.

Five virgins were not chosen because they did not have enough oil. They had some oil, but not enough! Indeed, there are many things that need to be in sufficient quantities if they are to be useful. Salt is one of them. There may be salt in food but if the salt is not enough, it is as though there is no salt in the food. You may work hard but if you do not work hard enough, your work may prove futile.

> Ye are the salt of the earth: but if the salt have lost his savour, wherewith shall it be salted? It is thenceforth good for nothing, but to be cast out, and to be trodden under foot of men.
>
> Matthew 5:13

Seven Things that Need to be Enough

1. **There should be enough churches.** There needs to be enough churches if you are to influence a nation. Having one church in a nation is not enough to make a strong impact on that nation.

2. **There should be enough prayer.** Saying three-minute prayers is not enough. Jesus prayed for three hours! Jesus prayed all night! Jesus waited on God for forty days and forty nights! Three-minute prayers cannot make an impact on your life and ministry. A pastor said to me, "I am not able to pray for more than twenty minutes." He continued, "I always marvel when you say that you pray for an hour."

3. **There should be enough missionaries.** If you send just a few missionaries into the world, they will not have enough of an impact.

4. **There should to be enough church buildings.** There must be enough church buildings littered along the countryside of a nation to give it the feeling of being a Christian nation. As you see temples of other religions scattered along the countryside, you get the feeling that the country is sold out to that religion.

5. **There should be enough money.** There must be enough money to do the work of God. If you do not have enough money, you cannot accomplish much! You may have some money but not enough to do the work of God. You will need to learn how to raise enough money to do the work of God!

6. **There should be enough books.** The reason why the Bible has such a great impact in the world is because it is the most published and printed book in the world. The more a book is published and the more it is printed, the more it is read!

7. **There needs to be enough waiting on God.** Waiting on God involves spending quality time with God. There are many ministers who do not make enough time to wait on God. Can you spend three days with God alone? Can you spend a whole day with God? The Levites were expected to spend seven days with God.

    And ye shall not go out of the door of the tabernacle of the congregation in seven days, until the days of your consecration be at an end: for seven days shall he consecrate you.

    Leviticus 8:33

Few Are Chosen because People Expect Someone to Do What They Should Do for Themselves

And the foolish said unto the wise, GIVE US OF YOUR OIL; FOR OUR LAMPS ARE GONE OUT. BUT THE WISE ANSWERED, SAYING, NOT SO; lest there be not enough for us and you: but GO YE RATHER TO THEM THAT SELL, AND BUY FOR YOURSELVES. And while they went to buy, the bridegroom came; and they that were ready went in with him to the marriage: and the door was shut.

Matthew 25:8-10

Many are called but few are chosen. Few end up being chosen because there are things that many people do not do in order to be chosen. In the story of the ten virgins, the foolish virgins expected the wise virgins to give some of their oil to them. It is foolish to expect someone to do for you what only you can do for yourself. The wise virgins said to the foolish virgins, "Go and get oil for yourselves." There are things you need to do for yourself that no one can do for you. In the ministry, people do not get chosen because, they expect someone else to do things for them that they should do for themselves.

Seven Things that You Have to Do for Yourself

1. **Examinations:** No one can pass your exams for you. You have to sit for an exam yourself. There are hard things you are going to have to do in order to pass your exams. No one can sit up in the night and study for you. No one can sit in the exam room and write your exam for you. No one can memorise things for you.

2. **Knowing the word of God:** No one can read your Bible for you. No one can memorise scriptures for you. No one can listen to messages for you. No one can study the Bible for you. No one can meditate on the word of God for you. No one can receive a revelation of the scripture for you. Indeed, knowing the word of God is something you have to do for yourself.

3. **Prayer:** No one can pray the prayers you need to pray for yourself. You need to relate with God yourself. You need to speak to God yourself. You need to lie on the floor and call on God yourself. Some people employ prayer warriors to pray for them. But nothing can replace the prayers you need to pray personally.

4. **Holiness:** No one can be holy for you. The scripture teaches that everyone must know how to possess his vessel in sanctification and honour (1 Thessalonians 4:4). No one

can fight fornication for you. No one can live a sanctified life for you. You are either sanctified or you are not.

5. **Humility:** No one can be humble for you. You are either humble or you are not. It is up to you to decide! The scripture teaches that we should humble ourselves (James 4:10). No one can go low for you. You have to do the things you have to do in order to humble yourself and go low. It is up to you! Be meek and lowly! We are all in danger of pride. Pride is an invisible and dangerous enemy. No one can humble himself on your behalf.

6. **Anointing:** No one can become anointed for you. No one can receive the Holy Spirit for you. You have to receive Him yourself. On the day of Pentecost, there were a hundred and twenty people in the Upper Room. When the Holy Ghost fell on them, there was a flame for every head (Acts 2:1-3). Indeed, there is a flame and an anointing for every single person. No one receives the Holy Spirit on behalf of someone else.

In 1988, I was waiting on God in a room in a small town called Suhum. I received the power of the Holy Spirit on my life and I heard a voice saying, "*From today you can teach.*" It was not the life and ministry of another person that changed. It was *my* life and ministry that changed. No one receives an anointing for you. You must receive it yourself!

You must rise up and receive the Holy Spirit for yourself. Decide to be one of the anointed few. No one can do that for you!

7. **Knowing God:** No one can know God for you. Relationships are things that depend on personal interactions. If you do not personally interact with God, you will not know Him. Apostle Paul said, "That I may know him and the power of his resurrection" (Philippians 3:10). Apostle Paul knew God. You cannot know God through someone. No one can do this for you! You can belong to a group that has very spiritual people in it. But if you do not fight to know

God, you will not know Him. Why is that? Because when someone knows God, it does not automatically make his friend also know God. You have to know God for yourself.

I have friends who do not know God. I even have friends who are atheists. The knowledge I have of God is not transmitted to them because they are my friends. It is time to have your own quiet time. Few are chosen because they do not have their own quiet time. Many are called but few are chosen because they do not spend time with God to know Him for themselves.

Many Christian groups exist but everyone within the group knows God to a different extent. Do not depend on the group culture. You must know God for yourself!

CHAPTER 10

Few Are Chosen because They Are Not Ready

And of the children of Issachar, which were MEN THAT HAD UNDERSTANDING OF THE TIMES, to know what Israel ought to do; the heads of them were two hundred; and all their brethren were at their commandment.

1 Chronicles 12:32

Many are called but few are chosen! Few are chosen because they are not ready when they should be ready. Readiness is an important spiritual quality. The virgins were not expecting the lord to arrive when he did. It is important that you make yourself ready.

One day, I was going for a crusade. There were about eight people travelling with me for this crusade. One of them was not ready when it was time to leave. I asked the driver to take off and we left without this person. This lady was surprised that she had been left behind. From that time onwards, she was never late for a crusade.

You see, readiness is an important quality in the ministry. Your time and the time of the Lord are not the same. A good soldier is ready all the time.

You may have been called to go along for the crusade. But if you are not ready on time, you will be left behind.

When Jesus approached the fig tree in Mark 11, He was hoping to find fruits. When he did not get any figs to eat that afternoon, He cursed the tree (Mark 11:12-14, 20-21).

You will be cursed when you do not have fruits ready at the time they are required. Some people feel God will require fruit from them when they are old. Some think God will require fruit from them in their middle age.

God can require fruit from you at any time. No one can tell when God will ask for fruit from you. Do you want a curse on your life? I don't think so! Be ready with your fruits all the time!

CHAPTER 11

Few Are Chosen because They Are Not Practical

Then shall the kingdom of heaven be likened unto ten virgins, which took their lamps, and went forth to meet the bridegroom. And five of them were wise, and five were foolish.

Matthew 25:1-2

Many are called and few are chosen because some of the people who are called are not practical about life and ministry. The fact that we are spiritual people does not mean we should not know how to do practical things. An anointed person must be practical and down to earth. You must roll up your sleeves and do normal everyday activities if you want things to work.

When God spoke to me to write a book, I carried on in the ministry, not really taking any steps to write the book. Then one day, the Lord said to me, "If you do not employ someone for the book writing, you are not serious about the instruction I gave you."

I immediately went ahead and employed someone to help me to write the books. Although this person was not able to do what I wanted, I had taken a practical step towards obeying God's commission. It is important to take practical steps to obey every commission given to you by God.

Because people are not practical, they do not know how to build anything. Many impractical people sit in their offices and receive invoices that make no sense. Because these leaders are detached from realities, they have no idea that they are being seriously cheated. If you are not practical, you will not know the real cost of things.

One day, I met a man of God who said God had told him to build a church. I watched as this gentleman spent one year looking for a contractor and three years in putting together various documents. Because he had no idea on how to practically build, he was unable to implement God's commission to him.

People who are not practical do not know how to prosper. When people are not practical and pragmatic they do not know how to save money.

One day, I met another man of God who said God had told him to put up a church building. He set up a board to raise funds for the church building. I watched in amazement as the board blundered on with their duties. They spent more money in setting up the board than was needed to start the building. Impractical men hesitate and falter when they are faced with massive tasks to accomplish.

One day, the board decided to embark on a fund-raising breakfast meeting. Just as I expected, the cost of the food was far more than the money they raised. Because they were not practical men who have actually raised money and built things before, they were unable to raise much money.

The board rather incurred a debt. The board of this church hesitated and dithered and staggered and floundered and struggled and wallowed and faltered until nothing was accomplished. Indeed, this board was not honest enough to acknowledge that they had spent more money on being a board than on accomplishing the mandate of their pastor.

The call of God in the hands of impractical people never works. Many are called but few are chosen! Few are chosen because many people are not practical. Only five virgins went for the dinner because the other five were not practical people. Is this what is going to happen to your life? Are you going to end up not accomplishing the will of God because your head is in the clouds?

CHAPTER 12

Few Virgins Are Chosen because They Do Not Focus on Invisible Things

And five of them were wise, and five were foolish. They that were foolish took their lamps, and took no oil with them:

Matthew 25:2-3

Many are called but few are chosen! For various reasons, few end up being chosen! In this story, we see ten virgins being invited to a wedding. Few ended up being chosen to actually participate in the wedding.

Few are chosen because most people focus on outward things. In the ministry, you must decide to focus on things that are not seen. The whole world lives to give a good impression on the outside. Everyone dresses up nicely and looks very posh on the outside.

People do not look that nice when they are at home. Children grow up learning to look good on the outside whilst they completely neglect the inside. Serving God is all about serving Him with your heart. No one can see your heart. God sees differently from the way man sees.

Man looks on the outward but God looks on the inward and on the heart. David was not even considered as an option by the prophet. God was angry with the prophet, Samuel, for looking at the outward appearance of Eliab to choose a king. The prophet Samuel, even though he was experienced, was looking at the height and the stature of David's brothers. He was probably also looking at their age.

But none of these things impress God. The only thing that impressed God was the heart that David had. That is how God sees! He looks at the heart and decides on people based on their hearts (1 Samuel 16:7).

Today, your ministry depends on invisible things; things that cannot be seen from the outside. God wants you to focus on the inner, deep, hidden aspects. Five virgins were cut out of the call of God because they focused on their dress, their decorations and everything else except one little hidden aspect – the oil.

On the outward they looked the same as everyone else. They had lamps! They had oil! They had a wedding dress! They were there on time! But when it came to the little hidden extra oil, five of them did not have it. Today, you must ask yourself what hidden aspect of your life is missing or faulty. God wants to use you greatly but the hidden aspects of your life must be corrected.

Is there jealousy? Is there hatred? Is there wickedness? Is there unforgiveness in you? These kinds of things are not visible but in the end, they will destroy you. Is there sin and wickedness in you? Is there emptiness in you? Is there bitterness in you?

Although no one can see them, they are the very things that will destroy your life and ministry. Today, God is calling you to turn around and focus on the hidden things.

Jesus spoke of three things that people do not usually see.

1. **Hidden prayer:** He said when you pray, go into your closet and pray quietly and secretly and He will reward you openly. Prayer is one of the hidden things that must be present in your life if you are to do well in God.

   But thou, when thou prayest, enter into thy closet, and when thou hast shut thy door, pray to thy Father which is in secret; and thy Father which seeth in secret shall reward thee openly.

   Matthew 6:6

2. **Hidden fasting:** He said when you fast do not let it be seen and known by everyone. It is one of the hidden things for which you will receive a reward. Your continual fasting and waiting on God will earn you many rewards in heaven.

   But thou, when thou fastest, anoint thine head, and wash thy face; That thou appear not unto men to fast, but unto thy Father which is in secret: and thy Father, which seeth in secret, shall reward thee openly.

   Matthew 6:17-18

3. **Hidden giving:** Jesus also spoke about giving. He said when you do your alms, do it secretly. Do not let your left hand know what your right hand is doing and you will receive a reward.

Therefore when thou doest thine alms, do not sound a trumpet before thee, as the hypocrites do in the synagogues and in the streets, that they may have glory of men. Verily I say unto you, they have their reward. But when thou doest alms, let not thy left hand know what thy right hand doeth:

Matthew 6:2-3

The five virgins who had extra oil hidden in their bags had the reward of going into the wedding. Indeed, it is the hidden unseen aspect of your life that will determine the level to which you will go.

Over the years I have observed various missionaries setting out to serve the Lord. Most of the ones who do not do well have something hidden in their lives that prevent them from doing well. It is not easy to pick up the hidden faults of missionaries. They are well concealed.

One day, one of our missionaries told me how he spent his afternoons.

"I spend the time watching films. Throughout the day, I watch movies and sleep in the afternoons."

Another missionary said, "I go to the internet café to do some office work."

He said guiltily, "Unfortunately, I watch pornography most of the time."

Obviously, these missionaries were not successful on the mission field. Whenever people are not successful on the mission field, there is something ominous hidden or tucked away somewhere.

Today, God is calling you to come out of darkness to be like the five virgins who were doing well on the outside and were also doing well on the inside where no one could see. Are you okay on the inside? Or are you just shining from the outside?

CHAPTER 13

Few Virgins Are Chosen because They Are Not Known by Jesus

But he answered and said, Verily I say unto you, I know you not.

Matthew 25:12

Five of the virgins were not known by the bridegroom. The master said, "I do not know you." It is important to be known! It is very important to be known! There are many people who choose to sit at the back, stay at the back and remain unknown. There are those who stand at the back and watch you from afar. There are those who, when they come into your presence, still remain silent and choose the furthermost position.

All these are evil practices that make you an unknown element. What are you doing to make yourself known in the church? What are you doing to make yourself known by Jesus? The first sin of Adam and Eve was to run away from God. Before they fell into sin, they were always happy to hear from the Lord God. They were always happy to fellowship with Him in the cool of the day.

It is important to do whatever you must do in order to be known. Staying at the back and being quiet is not a good thing. There is nothing you can hide from God. Allow yourself to be known! Allow yourself to be assessed! Allow yourself to be exposed! It will only help you to become a better person. Stop running away into the shadows! Stop hiding between the trees. The five virgins were rejected because the master said, "I do not know you!"

Being known is one of the most important spiritual achievements you can ever attain to. In heaven, even our thoughts are broadcast. In heaven, there is no sun. There are no shadows. The presence of the Lord is the light we have. In heaven, there is no murky water. The river of life is crystal clear. Everything is seen.

John said, "If we walk in the light, we have fellowship one with another" (1 John 1:7). You will never achieve real fellowship until you are known as you really are.

Stop hiding! Stop pretending! Stop trying to give a great impression of yourself. We are all made of mud and dust. We are all struggling to serve the Lord. God will help us to get to the end of this journey by His supernatural power.

CHAPTER 14

Few Servants Are Chosen because They Are Not Occupied with the Work

And as they heard these things, he added and spake a parable, because he was nigh to Jerusalem, and because they thought that the kingdom of God should immediately appear. He said therefore, A certain nobleman went into a far country to receive for himself a kingdom, and to return. AND HE CALLED HIS TEN SERVANTS, AND DELIVERED THEM TEN POUNDS, AND SAID UNTO THEM, OCCUPY TILL I COME. But his citizens hated him, and sent a message after him, saying, We will not have this man to reign over us.

And it came to pass, that when he was returned, having received the kingdom, then he commanded these servants to be called unto him, to whom he had given the money, that he might know how much every man had gained by trading.

Then came the first, saying, Lord, thy pound hath gained ten pounds. And he said unto him, Well, thou good servant: because thou hast been faithful in a very little, have thou authority over ten cities. And the second came, saying, Lord, thy pound hath gained five pounds. And he said likewise to him, Be thou also over five cities.

And another came, saying, Lord, behold, here is thy pound, which I have kept laid up in a napkin: For I feared thee, because thou art an austere man: thou takest up that thou layedst not down, and reapest that thou didst not sow. And he saith unto him, Out of thine own mouth will I judge thee, thou wicked servant. Thou knewest that I was an austere man, taking up that I laid not down, and reaping that I did not sow: Wherefore then gavest not thou my money into the bank, that at my coming I might have required mine own with usury?

And he said unto them that stood by, Take from him the pound, and give it to him that hath ten pounds. (And they said unto him, Lord, he hath ten pounds.)

For I say unto you, That unto every one which hath shall be given; and from him that hath not, even that he hath shall be taken away from him. But those mine enemies, which would not that I should reign over them, bring hither, and slay them before me.

Luke 19:11-27

Many are called but few are chosen! Why is this? Many people are given the Great Commission by the Lord but few end up being chosen because they do not make themselves fully occupied with the Commission. Jesus said to His servants, "Occupy till I come." "Occupy till I come" means make yourselves busy till I come. When you are not busy with the work of the Lord, all kinds of ideas will come to you. It is important that we fill our time and our lives with the mission that God has given us.

Why are you alive? You are alive to fulfil the commands and instructions of the Lord. The difference between you and the wild animals on the earth, is in the fact that God has given you a commission! The wild animals have no commission. All they do is to spend their lives eating, drinking, fighting and giving birth. Since you are not a wild animal, God has given you a Great Commission. He has given you something to live for.

Perhaps you are called to the ministry! Perhaps God wants you to be a pastor, an evangelist or an apostle. It is sad to see how many ministers do not give themselves wholly to becoming the best evangelists or apostles that they could be. It is sad to see pastors who do not give themselves to develop the art of growing churches.

It is sad to see apostles who do not give themselves to develop the art of planting churches. It is sad to see apostles who do not have the vision of planting thousands of churches. It is sad to see evangelists who do not give themselves to winning as many souls as possible. The fields of harvest lie there, waiting for true evangelists to arrive and come to the rescue of the dying souls in the world.

There are people that are called to be teachers but do not give themselves to the art of teaching. Many of us are simply not occupied with the task that God has given to us. We have not occupied our lives with the great work that has been presented to us. As a medical doctor, I can tell you that it is far more difficult to be a pastor than to be doctor. It is far more difficult to be an apostle than to be a medical doctor.

It is time to give ourselves wholly to the great call of God that is before us. Many of us would shine like stars if we were to give ourselves wholly to this work. Today, it looks as though few are chosen in the way Reinhard Bonnke was chosen to be an evangelist. It looks as though few are chosen in the way Yonggi Cho was chosen to build a big church. It looks as though few are chosen to become prophets and teachers, like the way Kenneth Hagin became a teacher of the Word. But it is not the case that few have been called. Indeed, many have been called but few are chosen because many do not occupy themselves with the call of God. It is time to occupy yourself with the call that you feel in your heart.

Years ago, I was standing under a big tree in a garden praying with some students. I told them that I had been called to be a teacher of the Word. My friend standing on the other side of the garden said he had also been called to be a minister. As the years went by, he gave himself to his profession and I gave myself to the ministry of the Lord Jesus. That is how come you are reading this book today.

If you occupy yourself with the call of God, you will find yourself shining. You will realise that God actually calls many people but few are chosen because few people occupy themselves with what God calls them to do.

Stand up today and do what God has told you to do! If God has told you to write songs, spend all your time writing songs, singing them and making them known to people. Occupy yourself with the call of God! You will shine like a star as you occupy yourself with what God has given you!

CHAPTER 15

Few Are Chosen because They Do Not Have Compassion on People

When the Son of man shall come in his glory, and all the holy angels with him, then shall he sit upon the throne of his glory: And before him shall be gathered all nations: and he shall separate them one from another, as a shepherd divideth his sheep from the goats: And he shall set the sheep on his right hand, but the goats on the left. Then shall the King say unto them on his right hand, Come, ye blessed of my Father, inherit the kingdom prepared for you from the foundation of the world: For I was an hungred, and ye gave me meat: I was thirsty, and ye gave me drink: I was a stranger, and ye took me in:

Matthew 25:31-35

Many are called but few are chosen! Why are only a few chosen? In this amazing scripture, Jesus teaches about how all the nations are summoned for judgment. Indeed, the nations are divided into two groups; sheep and goats.

At the beginning, all the sheep and all the goats were called to the Lord's presence. In the end, only the sheep were selected. What was the basis of the selection of these sheep? The "sheep" nations are the nations that had compassion on the people of this world. If you want to be used by God, it is important to have compassion on people with problems in this world.

Being a physics teacher or a chemistry teacher is different from being a minister of the gospel. A physics teacher does not need to have compassion if he wants to be successful. A chemistry teacher does not need compassion to do his work. A minister of the gospel needs to have compassion on the people to whom he has been sent. If you want to serve God properly, you need to be filled with the compassion of the Lord.

But when he saw the multitudes, he was moved with compassion on them, because they fainted, and were scattered abroad, as sheep having no shepherd.

Matthew 9:36

Jesus went about preaching, teaching and healing. He did this because He was filled with compassion for the people. Many are called by the Lord but few are able to develop the compassion that they need to be successful and fruitful in ministry. All the nations which were set aside as "goat" nations are the nations which did not have compassion on people's problems and difficulties.

Today, there are many people who are homeless, hungry, thirsty and sick. You do not have to be sick or in great difficulty yourself before you remember all these situations. God's will for us is to be filled with compassion for those who cannot help themselves.

Souls are parting to eternity! Souls are perishing every day! By midnight today, many thousands would have died and gone to hell for ever. How many people will die in Christ? How many will live again? Do you care? Do you have any feelings?

Do you wonder about what happens to all the lost souls in this world?

Without compassion you cannot be a good evangelist. A good evangelist has compassion on the souls that he is preaching to. He does not just rattle out a message that he has learnt from Bible school. He is filled with feelings and compassion for the lost and the dying.

A good pastor is filled with love. He feels for the difficulties that his sheep have. He loves the members that God brings to him. He cares for them deeply and wants them to do well. A good shepherd wants the sheep to be happy, to have good marriages and to have a good life. Without compassion, without a certain kind of feeling you can never be a good pastor.

Today, God is calling you to be filled with compassion. He is calling you to be filled with the feeling that you need to be a good minister. Scripture teaches us that Jesus was touched with the feeling of our infirmity. If you do not have these feelings, you are not a true minister.

Watch out for people who hold the Bible, who stand in the pulpit but have no feelings for the people they are speaking to. Watch out for dry, emotionless, flat, prosaic ministers who speak religious words that are not understood by most people.

Why do you preach messages that no one understands? Why do you not care for the people you are speaking to? How can you speak to them in a language they do not understand?

Today, God is calling you to develop the feeling of compassion. How can you develop this feeling of compassion? I think you should pray for compassion. I think you should call on God to give you a feeling of compassion for the people. It is a supernatural thing to have the compassion of God.

CHAPTER 16

Few Are Chosen because Their Riches Deceive Them

And, behold, one came and said unto him, Good Master, what good thing shall I do, that I may have eternal life? And he said unto him, Why callest thou me good? There is none good but one, that is, God: but if thou wilt enter into life, keep the commandments. He saith unto him, which? Jesus said, Thou shalt do no murder, Thou shalt not commit adultery, Thou shalt not steal, Thou shalt not bear false witness, Honour thy father and thy mother: and, Thou shalt love thy neighbour as thyself.

The young man saith unto him, all these things have I kept from my youth up: what lack I yet?

Jesus said unto him, If thou wilt be perfect, go and sell that thou hast, and give to the poor, and thou shalt have treasure in heaven: and come and follow me.

But when the young man heard that saying, he went away sorrowful: for he had great possessions.

THEN SAID JESUS UNTO HIS DISCIPLES, VERILY I SAY UNTO YOU, THAT A RICH MAN SHALL HARDLY ENTER INTO THE KINGDOM OF HEAVEN. And again I say unto you, It is easier for a camel to go through the eye of a needle, than for a rich man to enter into the kingdom of God.

When his disciples heard it, they were exceedingly amazed, saying, who then can be saved?

Matthew 19:16-25

Many are called! Indeed, if many are called, some rich people will also be called.

This rich man was ready to do almost everything to follow Jesus. Unfortunately, he was not ready to give up his riches and follow Jesus Christ.

Jesus said to him, "If you want to be perfect you must give up your riches and follow me." The rich man was unable to give up everything to follow Jesus. Few are chosen because many people are deceived by their riches.

I would have had many more missionaries and pastors if it were not for the riches many decided to follow.

Riches are deceptive! Money is deceptive! Money tells lies and makes you feel it will take care of you. Money is deceptive!

Money makes you feel that it is all you need! Because of money, opportunities and jobs many people do not enter the ministry. The love of riches is one of the greatest things that reduce the number of people who are eventually chosen.

Do not think that God only chooses poor people. Do not think that God calls only poor wretches who have no substance in this life. God calls rich people! God calls educated people! God also calls people who have a great potential to generate wealth. Unfortunately, many who are called shun the calling in exchange for potential riches that they may have and the opportunities that are before them.

As the years go by, many of these promises for wealth and great potential end up as nothing. By the time people are too old and unable to obey the call of God, they realize that they have been deceived by the riches. Many are called! Many rich people are called! Hardly do rich people heed the call of God! Hardly do rich people obey the call! And hardly do rich people get chosen for the high things of ministry!

Today is your day to set aside the promise of riches that comes from this world. Jesus is promising you far greater riches in eternity. Jesus is promising you golden crowns and streets of gold, with honours and rewards that will last throughout eternity.

You will never regret choosing the Lord over money. You will never regret serving Jesus instead of serving mammon.

You cannot love two masters. Today, God is imparting to you a hatred for money and love for God! I am sad to say that many people have love for money and hatred for God. If I told you that you hated God, you are not likely to believe me. But Jesus said you could not have two masters. You will love one and hate the other! (Luke 16:13).

One day I was counselling a brother who seemed to have two masters. I told him that he hated me. He denied hating me vehemently. But I pointed out the scripture to him: you cannot love two masters. You either love one or hate the other! I told him that he loved the other master and hated me. Sometimes it is difficult to accept that you have hatred in you. Most lay pastors do not accept that they hate God. But you cannot love God and love money as well. You either love one or hate the other.

The one you obey is the one you really love! The one you follow is the one you really love! The one you trust is the one you really love! The one you talk to is the one you really love!

Today, you must accept the fact that loving God is not compatible with loving money. You must choose what you want to serve. You must not allow riches to deceive you and turn you away from your great Saviour and God.

Jesus is everything! Jesus died for you!

It is worth serving the Lord! It is worth following Jesus!

Let your love be with Jesus and not with anything else!

CHAPTER 17

Few Are Chosen because They Make Excuses

Then said he unto him, a certain man made a great supper, and bade many:

And sent his servant at supper time to say to them that were bidden, Come; for all things are now ready. And they all with one consent began to make excuse. The first said unto him, I have bought a piece of ground, and I must needs go and see it: I pray thee have me excused. And another said, I have bought five yoke of oxen, and I go to prove them: I pray thee have me excused. And another said, I have married a wife, and therefore I cannot come.

So that servant came, and shewed his lord these things. Then the master of the house being angry said to his servant, Go out quickly into the streets and lanes of the city, and bring in hither the poor, and the maimed, and the halt, and the blind. And the servant said, Lord, it is done as thou hast commanded, and yet there is room. And the lord said unto the servant, Go out into the highways and hedges, and compel them to come in, that my house may be filled.

For I say unto you, That none of those men which were bidden shall taste of my supper.

Luke 14:16-24

Many are called to this amazing dinner! Jesus invites many people to the great supper. You would have thought that everyone would simply drop everything and attend the great supper. But it is not so! Many people come up with excuses when it comes to God. As you become experienced in the work of God you realise that an excuse is a sign of someone who does not want to serve the Lord. God is calling you today to love Him, to serve Him and obey Him with all your heart. Drop every excuse and you will become one of the chosen few.

Why is it that so few end up being chosen? Some people give excuses about the land that they have bought and the properties that they are investing in. Others give excuses about their jobs - the oxen that they are using to plough the fields. Others give reasons that are connected to their marriages. Someone said that, "I have married a wife. I cannot come." These are the three big types of excuses that persist until today.

God has greater things in store for you. There is someone reading this book: you would have been in Japan preaching the gospel and having great experiences all over the world, but you made excuses about your job. You made excuses related to marriage. You made excuses in relation to your accumulation of wealth. These excuses have taken you away from the call of God. Beginning from now, some people are going to break away from the myriad of excuses.

Stop delaying! Stop lying to yourself! Stop deceiving everyone around you! Get out of the grip of these terrible excuses and serve the Lord today. Do not use your wife as a reason any more! Don't use your husband as a reason any more! Don't use your business as a reason any more! God is calling you to serve Him with joy and I see you rising up in the ministry!

CHAPTER 18

Few Are Chosen because They Do Not Communicate Properly

Not every one that saith unto me, Lord, Lord, shall enter into the kingdom of heaven; but he that doeth the will of my Father which is in heaven. Many will say to me in that day, Lord, Lord, have we not prophesied in thy name? And in thy name have cast out devils? And in thy name done many wonderful works? AND THEN WILL I PROFESS UNTO THEM, I NEVER KNEW YOU: depart from me, ye that work iniquity.

Matthew 7:21-23

Many are called but few are chosen because they do not communicate properly.

Few are chosen because they do not have a good relationship with God. Most people do not communicate properly and therefore do not have good relationships. There is no way to know people who do not communicate. They remain unknown to God and to us. Communication is the only way to develop a relationship with someone.

Do you want to hear those words "I never knew you"? God wants to know you! God wants to be your friend! The words, "I never knew you" are going to be used as a basis for rejecting people. I know you were thinking that God would say, "You were never pure." "You were never holy." "You did not abstain from fornication."

God is saying, "I never knew you." God needs to know you! God needs to be close to you! God wants to have a relationship with you! When God has a good relationship with you, you are safe.

All through the years I have been sending people to the mission field. There is one characteristic that stands out. Those who communicate properly are the ones who have done well on the mission field. Not communicating well is the greatest problem of unsuccessful missionaries. Not knowing the people that you have sent out is the greatest difficulty and problem of ministers.

On many occasions, I have had to select people for a mission. On several occasions the basis for my non-selection has been "I don't know this person and I don't know that person." I have filtered people out because I did not know them. Knowing and being known is critical to serving God.

How can I know God? How can I be known by God? You can know God by talking to Him. You can know God by praying from your heart. When you pray you are speaking to God. When you are speaking from your heart, you get close to someone. As you wait on God and speak to Him from your heart, God will also speak to you. Gradually, you will form a close bond and close ties with God. Your heart to heart conversations with God will win Him over. God wants to relate with you.

When Joseph died, a new pharaoh arose. The children of Israel suffered greatly. They prayed! They cried! They hoped!

And it came to pass in process of time, that the king of Egypt died: and the children of Israel sighed by reason of the bondage, and they cried, and THEIR CRY CAME UP UNTO GOD by reason of the bondage. And GOD HEARD their groaning, and GOD REMEMBERED his covenant with Abraham, with Isaac, and with Jacob. And GOD LOOKED upon the children of Israel, and GOD HAD RESPECT unto them.

Exodus 2:23-25

You will notice that the cry of the children of Israel came up onto God. You will notice the response it evoked from God.

You will notice that God heard!

You will notice that God remembered!

You will notice that God looked!

You will notice that God had respect unto them!

God really responds to your cry! God really listens to all that you are saying!

CHAPTER 19

Few Are Chosen because They Are Workers of Iniquity

Strive to enter in at the strait gate: for many, I say unto you, will seek to enter in, and shall not be able. When once the master of the house is risen up, and hath shut to the door, and ye begin to stand without, and to knock at the door, saying, Lord, Lord, open unto us; and he shall answer and say unto you, I know you not whence ye are: Then shall ye begin to say, We have eaten and drunk in thy presence, and thou hast taught in our streets. But he shall say, I tell you, I KNOW YOU NOT WHENCE YE ARE; DEPART FROM ME, ALL YE WORKERS OF INIQUITY. There shall be weeping and gnashing of teeth, when ye shall see Abraham, and Isaac, and Jacob, and all the prophets, in the kingdom of God, and you yourselves thrust out.

Luke 13:24-28

Many are called but few are chosen. Why are few chosen? Why few are chosen is the big question we are seeking to answer in this book. The scripture above shows that few are chosen because people are workers of iniquity.

Sin is the reason why many people are eliminated from the ministry. It may sound quite simple but it is the truth. Over the years I have come to see that there is always a kind of sin lurking somewhere in those who do not do well in the ministry. Sin is like a mysterious disease! It destroys our lives in a mystical way. This is why the scripture speaks of the mystery of iniquity.

For the mystery of iniquity doth already work: only he who now letteth will let, until he be taken out of the way.

2 Thessalonians 2:7

Iniquity is mysterious because it does not seem to have the same effect on everyone. Not everyone who steps into immorality dies suddenly. Many people live in sin for years and nothing seems to happen to them. Other people seem to sin and within a sort while their lives seem to be engulfed in a curse.

People drop out because they engage in iniquity that they should not engage in. Iniquity eliminates many of the people who are called.

1. **The iniquity of lying and deception.** If you want to last long in the ministry you have to get rid of your lying tendencies. Ministry means truth from the heart. You shall know the truth and the truth shall make you free (John 8:32).

   He that worketh deceit shall not dwell within my house: he that telleth lies shall not tarry in my sight.

   Psalm 101:7

2. **The iniquity of immorality.** Many ministers are involved in immorality. Since we are born into a very sexual body, there are tendencies to swing out of the narrow way and become perverted.

Today, God is delivering you from the iniquity of immorality! This iniquity is mysterious because there does not seem to be the same response from heaven regarding it. I know there are people who have successfully run their ministries for years whilst living in sin. On the other hand, there are those who make one mistake and are catapulted into a crisis. This is why it is called the mystery of iniquity.

3. **The iniquity of rebellion.** The mystery of disobedience and rebellion is released in the church. Many ministers are in disobedience and open rebellion to God. Disobedience is the trigger that releases most curses. Decide to be a man of obedience. To obey is even better than to sacrifice! (1 Samuel 15:22)

CHAPTER 20

Few Are Chosen because the Seeds Fell by the Way Side

And he spake many things unto them in parables, saying, Behold, a sower went forth to sow; And when he sowed, some seeds fell by the way side, and the fowls came and devoured them up: Some fell upon stony places, where they had not much earth: and forthwith they sprung up, because they had no deepness of earth: And when the sun was up, they were scorched; and because they had no root, they withered away.

And some fell among thorns; and the thorns sprung up, and choked them: But other fell into good ground, and brought forth fruit, some an hundredfold, some sixtyfold, some thirtyfold.

Matthew 13:3-8

Many seeds are sown by the sower. Indeed, many seeds are sown but few seeds germinate and become anything. Why is it that many of the seeds that are sown amount to nothing?

One of the reasons is because the seeds fall by the wayside. Do not allow yourself to belong to the wayside parts of the ministry. If you belong to a church decide to be in the mainstream of the church. If you belong to a choir decide to be in the mainstream of the choir. If you belong to a fellowship decide to be in the mainstream of the fellowship. In everything you do, decide to be in the mainstream.

Do not accept to be an outsider. The wayside is a dangerous place to be. When you are by the wayside, the wicked one will come and steal the Word from you.

What is it that makes you an outsider? Why are you an outsider? Decide not to be an outsider. Decide not to be a deviant. Decide to come closer and be part of the mainstream. Do not allow the devil to tell you that you are an outsider.

One day I met someone whom God had called to work with me. Unknown to me, someone had been poisoning this worker with an evil seed. This person was told over and over again, that he was an outsider. It is not easy to be an outsider. Outsiders easily become Judases. Judas was an outsider. He was the only disciple who was not from Galilee. As Jesus was loving His disciples, Judas was developing a complex. Outsiders always develop a complex. Outsiders interpret things differently and wrongly.

CHAPTER 21

Few Are Chosen because They Are Not Deep

Now the parable is this: The seed is the word of God. Those by the way side are they that hear; then cometh the devil, and taketh away the word out of their hearts, lest they should believe and be saved. They on the rock are they, which, when they hear, receive the word with joy; AND THESE HAVE NO ROOT, which for a while believe, and in time of temptation fall away.

Luke 8:11-13

Many are called but few are chosen! Why is it that few seeds germinate? Why is it that few seeds are successful at becoming mighty trees? Indeed, many seeds are sown but few seeds germinate and become something.

A man can produce as many as a hundred million sperms per millilitre. Out of all these millions of sperms, only one is needed to fertilize the egg. Indeed, many are called and few are chosen! If a woman gives birth to fraternal twins, it means that only two sperms out of several millions were chosen.

Few are chosen because many do not go deep enough. Many of the sperms do not go deep enough. Many of the sperms drop by the wayside. Some are even spilled outside. Such wayside sperms do not stand a chance of being useful.

It is time to go deeper! It is time to go deeper! What are you doing for God? What has God told you to do? Go deep into your calling!

How to Go Deeper

1. **Go deeper by having a big vision:** Decide to be the best minister of the gospel in your category. Your vision makes you. You do not make your vision. If you have a vision to be a very great minister of God, you will be forced to go deep into your calling.

2. **Go deeper by reading books about your ministry:** Read books about your calling. If you want to go deep in your ministry, you must read books that are connected to your ministry. When I wanted to have church growth, I read all sorts of books about church growth. I read books that had been written by every category of minister. Even books from other denominations were swallowed whole. The reason why you are not deep into your calling is because you do not read books that are specifically related to your calling.

3. **Go deeper by listening to specific messages:** Are you not tired of listening to the same wishy-washy messages about prosperity and success? You can go deeper into the ministry by listening to messages that will challenge you and take you deeper. I used to love Christian television. But at a point, I was unable to listen much to Christian television. I could not find anything deep enough. Nothing could take me deep enough.

Dear friend, there are deeper things that you will benefit from if you expose yourself to them. As you get deeper in God and into your calling, you will bear much fruit. Soon people will realise that you are one of the few who are chosen.

CHAPTER 22

Few Are Chosen because They Are Choked

And that which fell among thorns are they, which, when they have heard, go forth, and ARE CHOKED with cares and riches and pleasures of this life, and bring no fruit to perfection.

Luke 8:14

Many ministers have received the call of God but few have actually become anything as a result of the call. The responsibilities of life choke the word of God and they become unfruitful. If you see a hundred trees standing, you must realise that thousands of seeds originally landed on that ground. You must realise that only a hundred trees came out of the effort of planting hundreds of thousands of seeds.

God is calling you to be one of the few who are chosen. To become one of the few who are chosen you must overcome the cares, riches and pleasures of this world! These things are not sins but they are powerful chokers of the call of God.

When God called me into the ministry, I had a new young wife and little children. How to care for this family presented a challenge to me. But I shrugged off the thoughts that came to my mind and persisted with the call of God. I did not allow the cares of having a family to choke my calling.

To be in the ministry, you must be ready to put these aside and press towards the mark of the high calling. Do not allow the promise of riches or the promise of wealth to mar your calling. Few are chosen because they give themselves to the chokers.

Even after people have been in the ministry for some years, they are still affected by the chokers. You can see substantial deviations from real ministry because of the riches and pleasures of this life. God continues to call you and give you higher instructions all the way to the very end of your life. At every stage, the call of God will be met with these chokers. Chokers are ready to quench any further call that you receive.

When God called me to start the evangelistic ministry the chokers surrounded me. There were questions; "Will I have enough money to carry out this evangelistic ministry?" The cares of this life multiplied: "Would I be able to take care of my family? Would I be able to take care of the churches? Would I be able to still do the ministry in the right way if I went on the evangelistic field?"

These were questions that I had to ask myself. As I carry on in ministry, the opportunity to give myself to relaxation and pleasures are everywhere. If I yield to these ideas, the call of God will be choked and everything will be different. It is time to realise the power of these chokers and resist them with all your might.

God has called you to do great things. You must finish your calling! You must rise up in the name of Jesus and go to the ends of the world. Do not let riches deceive you! Riches are very deceptive! Riches are always trying to redirect you away from the will of God. Riches are always trying to deceive you and tell you that there is something better, something higher and something else worth giving yourself for.

There is nothing worth exchanging your calling for! There are more fruits that you can bear. There are more places that you can go to. There are more things you can do. There are more books you can write. There are more crusades you can hold. There are more conferences you can be part of.

It is time to obey the call of God. Do not let pleasure hold you back. I have seen ministers of God who are only prepared to travel to places which have five-star hotels. They must have special dinners. They must drink wine. They must be treated like kings and princes all the time. They are not prepared to live anywhere or do the work of God without all these fancy pleasures.

It is time to say "Yes" to the call of God, and to resist with all your might everything that chokes the call of God!

CHAPTER 23

Few Are Chosen because of Their Desires

Now these things were our examples, to the intent WE SHOULD NOT LUST after evil things, as they also lusted.

1 Corinthians 10:6

Many Israelites left Egypt heading for the Promised Land. Many were called to the Promised Land. Only Joshua, Caleb and the youth finally made it to the Promised Land. The story of the Israelites leaving Egypt to the Promised Land is a classic example of how many were called but few were chosen. It reveals many of the reasons why few people make it to the high places that God has destined for them.

Many are called to the ministry. Perhaps you are one of the many who are called to the ministry. Unfortunately, it seems that only a few are chosen. One of the reasons why few people make it is because of their lusts.

There are many lusts that ministers have. It is the lusts of other things that drown the call of God. In the parable of the sower, Jesus explained that those who have lusts for other things are not able to bear much fruit.

And the cares of this world, and the deceitfulness of riches, and the lusts of other things entering in, choke the word, and it becometh unfruitful.

Mark 4:19

The lusts that you have are very important. Scripture teaches us that if anyone loves the world, the love of the Father is not in him (1 John 2:15). When you love the world you cannot love God. What is in the world? The things that are in the world are the lust of the flesh, the lust of the eyes and the pride of life. The world is full of people who are running after their lusts. They desire many fleshly things. The world is full of people who are filled with the lust of the eyes. They have set their eyes on many things and are following them with all their heart. The world is full of people who want things that make them proud in this life.

For all that is in the world, the lust of the flesh, and the lust of the eyes, and the pride of life, is not of the Father, but is of the world.

1 John 2:16

To serve God is to love the Father. Loving the Father means that all these lusts cannot flourish or thrive in you. It is important for every minister to search his heart and see what kind of lusts are in him. What do you desire?

One minister said to me, " I like money."

I thought to myself, "This person is not going to go very far with God."

Another minister clearly showed his desire for cars. He said, "I like cars. I love to have different kinds of cars."

Other men of God desire to be in Europe or America. The lusts of other things always quench the call of God. I remember a man of God who started a church. His ministry flourished and many people attended his services. The church prospered so much that they were able to buy a bus.

This bus was used to bring church members to church and also to bring instruments to the church. They painted a big banner on the church: "Victory. Success. Glory". As the victory, success and glory continued in this church, the pastor applied for a visa to go to America. He had never travelled outside his home country.

The victory, success and glory continued to work and he received a visa to the United States of America. The whole church prayed for their pastor as he went on his first missionary journey to America. The trip was supposed to last six weeks. Unfortunately, when this brother saw the lights, the buildings and the glittering glitzy riches of America he was completely overwhelmed. The "Victory. Success. Glory" church waited for him for weeks on end but he did not return. Believe it or not, this brother was completely overwhelmed by his desire for the wealth of the western world. He never returned to his "Victory. Success. Glory" church!

It is true that the lusts of other things really does quench the call of God. Desire is a very important force. Whatever desire is within you will have an effect on your life! When God wanted to punish Eve, He put a desire in her. God knew that that desire would drive her along a certain road and she would feel the pain and punishment for the rest of her life. God said, "Your desire will be for a man and he will rule over you" (Genesis 3:16). Eve's desire for a man has been her greatest source of pain throughout the centuries. Women's desire for men has been their undoing. Their desire for husbands, their desire for children, their desire to be with someone, no matter who he is, has often been the source of pain for women.

Desire is a powerful thing. Always check your heart and see what kind of desires are working in your life.

God has called you to serve him but your lust of other things can quench and destroy that calling.

The children of Israel were on their way to the Promised Land. They overcame the Red Sea and many miracles had happened in Egypt. But their desires for other things – their lusts – completely derailed their opportunity to go to the Promised Land.

Today, God is calling you. Perhaps you have a desire to be in America. Perhaps you have a desire to have a British passport. Perhaps you have a desire to marry a fair-coloured lady. Perhaps you have a desire to marry a handsome, charming prince. Perhaps you have a desire to have a large family with six children. Perhaps you have a desire to drive a Mercedes Benz or a BMW. Today, God is warning you about your desires. Any of these desires could derail your calling.

Beware of the desires and the lusts that are within your soul! One day, they may spring up like a cobra and bite you in the face. You will find yourself destroyed just because you had some wrong desires.

Lusting after other things is like lusting after snakes. As you play with these evil creatures, do not be surprised if one of them bites you. Do not be surprised if one of these desires ends your calling and ministry.

CHAPTER 24

Few Are Chosen because of Their Idols

NEITHER BE YE IDOLATERS, as were some of them; as it is written, the people sat down to eat and drink, and rose up to play.

1 Corinthians 10:7

Many were called to the Promised Land but few actually entered because of idolatry. Idolatry is as real today as it was in the days of the Israelites. Almost every king of Israel had some kind of idol in his life. It is only king David and one other king who did not have an idol. Do not think that idolatry is a sin of the Old Testament. The New Testament warns us to keep ourselves from idols.

Little children, keep yourselves from idols. Amen.

1 John 5:21

What are the idols today? Idols are things that are alternatives to God. The idols of today are money, jobs and opportunities. Anything that makes you rise up early and work hard is a type of idol. Anything that you obey is a type of idol. Anything that you yield yourself to and follow with all your heart is an idol. Anything that you yield yourself to, more than you yield yourself to God is an idol. Why is that? Anything that is an alternative to Almighty God is an idol.

One day, I asked some people to go to the mission field and start a church. But they were not prepared to do so. These people who were unwilling to give themselves to the mission field, travelled to America and Europe for work. There, they were prepared to live in a cold and difficult environment for many years to earn more money. Indeed, after working for some time, some of them were transferred to African nations on missions. They went on missions to difficult African nations for the organisation that they worked for. They were prepared to do these things for the international organisations that they worked for, but not for God.

An idol is something you yield yourself to, more than you yield yourself to God. Some of these people were also sent to live in "mission countries" without their families. For several years they lived and survived without their families. They were prepared to do anything for these international organisations. At other times, some of them were sent to dangerous war zones. Anything you yield yourself to, more than you yield yourself to God is an idol!

Today, people rise up early and watch pornography for hours. People have boyfriends and girlfriends whom they travel to visit. They make great sacrifices and spend time and money with these lovers. But they are not prepared to spend a few days at a church camp. It is important to ask yourself what you yield yourself to. Whom do you sacrifice to and what do you sacrifice for? God notices these things and they offend him greatly.

Anyone you love more than you love God has taken the place of God and is becoming an idol. Get ready for God to strike that thing out of your life! Today, some Christians have elevated the love of a husband and the love of a wife above their love for God.

It is as though their marriage is the most important thing. They say things like, "God first, family second, ministry third." I do not find this in the Bible. It is one of the humanistic ideals that are being propagated by a backslidden church. God is always first and your service to God is always more important than anything else.

Jesus put His love for His disciples and those who obey God above His love for His mother and brethren. (Mark 3:33-35). Loving God is the greatest commandment! Anything that takes away your love for God becomes a curse. Husbands loving their wives more than they love God is a form of idolatry. Wives loving their husbands more than they love God is a form of idolatry. Pastors loving their churches and ministries more than they love God is a form of idolatry. Be careful that you do not offend God. Almighty God is the Creator of heaven and earth. One of the things He seeks for is for those who love Him.

The greatest commandment is to love God. Loving God is the only thing you can do to impress God. Loving God is the one thing you can do! When you give your love to something else, God notices it. Turn away from idolatry and you will become one of the few who are chosen.

Many pastors are called to serve the Lord. Do they really love God or do they love the cars they have gotten through the ministry? Do they really love God or they love the privileges, the adulation and the praises of men that they have gotten through the ministry?

It is time to love the Lord with all your heart! It is time to turn away from any alternative or substitute for God. Be careful of "God substitutes"! Be careful of things that are idol alternatives to your love for the Father!

CHAPTER 25

Few Are Chosen because of Fornication

Neither let us commit FORNICATION, as some of them committed, and fell in one day three and twenty thousand.

1 Corinthians 10:8

The children of Israel marched out of Egypt full of confidence in God. The children of Israel marched out of Egypt with their eyes on the Promised Land. They knew God had called them. They knew they were going to the land flowing with milk and honey. Unfortunately, very few of the original group made it to the Promised Land. Why is this?

Fornication was one of the clear reasons why many did not make it to the Promised Land. Many of the men and the women became embroiled in immorality. Their spiritual journey was cut short. Will our spiritual journey be cut short?

Fornication is one of the commonest sins in the world today. As the world has become more sinful, fornication has become almost as common as lying. Because this sin is so common, many ministers have minimised its significance in their minds. Many are called but few are chosen because of their sexual mistakes!

1. **Fornication is not supposed to be mentioned even once.** We do not have this warning about other sins. There is no scripture that says lying should not be mentioned even once. There is no scripture that says jealousy should not be mentioned even once. The Bible is very clear that fornication should not be mentioned even once.

   But fornication, and all uncleanness, or covetousness, let it not be once named among you, as becometh saints;

   Ephesians 5:3

2. **Fornication is the reason for the anger of God that comes on ministers.** God is angry with those whom He has called because of this sin. Paul said, "Do not let anybody deceive you with vain words," God's standard has not changed.

   But fornication, and all uncleanness, or covetousness, let it not be once named among you, as becometh saints; neither filthiness, nor foolish talking, nor jesting, which are not convenient: but rather giving of thanks. For this ye know, that no whoremonger, nor unclean person, nor covetous man, who is an idolater, hath any inheritance in the kingdom of Christ and of God. Let no man deceive you with vain words: for because of these things cometh the wrath of God upon the children of disobedience.

Ephesians 5:3-6

3. **Fornication is a sin against your body.** Fornication is something that harms your body. Perhaps this is why many diseases are released to the human race through sexual intercourse. Many diseases are released against God's servants because of their sin of fornication. Many lives are cut short because of fornication.

Neither let us commit fornication, as some of them committed, and fell in one day three and twenty thousand.

1 Corinthians 10:8

4. **Fornication is prevented by a personal revelation.** You will fight against fornication and prevent it through your personal efforts. Your efforts to fight fornication must be fierce and resolute. Everyone may have a different method of preventing fornication. If you do not fight extremes with extremes, you will only have yourself to blame.

That EVERY ONE OF YOU SHOULD KNOW HOW TO POSSESS HIS VESSEL in sanctification and honour; not in the lust of concupiscence, even as the Gentiles which know not God:

1 Thessalonians 4:4-5

5. **Fornication is prevented by having a good marriage.** Unfortunately, many Christians get married and do not have sex. This effort by satan to prevent couples from having sex, neutralizes the power that marriage has to prevent fornication.

Nevertheless, to *avoid* fornication, let every man have his own wife, and let every woman have her own husband. Let the husband render unto the wife due benevolence: and likewise also the wife unto the husband.

1 Corinthians 7:2-3

6. **Fornication is an act of despising God.** God is dishonoured through your fornication. It is not a wise thing to despise God. He that despises God will be lightly esteemed by God! (1 Samuel 2:30).

That every one of you should know how to possess his vessel in sanctification and honour; not in the lust of concupiscence, even as the Gentiles which know not God:

That no *man* go beyond and defraud his brother in *any* matter: because that the Lord is the avenger of all such, as we also have forewarned you and testified. FOR GOD HATH NOT CALLED US UNTO UNCLEANNESS, BUT UNTO HOLINESS. HE THEREFORE THAT DESPISETH, DESPISETH NOT MAN, BUT GOD, WHO HATH ALSO GIVEN UNTO US HIS HOLY SPIRIT.

1 Thessalonians 4:4-8

7. **Fornication and adultery will provoke God to revenge for those who have been robbed.** Be careful of falling into the wrath of God. God will destroy you practically because you have defrauded your Christian brother.

That no man go beyond and defraud his brother in any matter: because that the Lord is the avenger of all such, as we also have forewarned you and testified.

1 Thessalonians 4:6

CHAPTER 26

Few Are Chosen because They Murmur

Neither murmur ye, as some of them also murmured, and were destroyed of the destroyer.

1 Corinthians 10:10

Many are called! Many Christians are murmurers, complainers and bitter gossips. Gossiping, murmuring, backbiting, maligning are things that incur the wrath of God. God has sent us to the world to preach the gospel. God has given us mighty tasks to accomplish in His name. He has sent us into the world. He expects us to do great things for Him. As God has sent us, He knows that there will be giants in the land. A giant represents an obstacle, a hindrance, a problem and a difficulty. God does not expect you to murmur against Him because of the problems and difficulties that have arisen.

> And they told him, and said, we came unto the land whither thou sentest us, and surely it floweth with milk and honey; and this is the fruit of it. Nevertheless the people be strong that dwell in the land, and the cities are walled, and very great: and moreover we saw the children of Anak there. The Amalekites dwell in the land of the south: and the Hittites, and the Jebusites, and the Amorites, dwell in the mountains: and the Canaanites dwell by the sea, and by the coast of Jordan.
>
> And Caleb stilled the people before Moses, and said, Let us go up at once, and possess it; for we are well able to overcome it. But the men that went up with him said, we be not able to go up against the people; for they are stronger than we. And they brought up an evil report of the land which they had searched unto the children of Israel, saying, The land, through which we have gone to search it, is a land that eateth up the inhabitants thereof; and all the people that we saw in it are men of a great stature. And THERE WE SAW THE GIANTS, THE SONS OF ANAK, WHICH COME OF THE GIANTS: AND WE WERE IN OUR OWN SIGHT AS GRASSHOPPERS, and so we were in their sight.
>
> Numbers 13:27-33

Murmuring against God happens when you murmur against His servants. When the children of Israel spoke against Moses, they were speaking against God. The Bible says that God heard it. God always noticed when they murmured (Numbers 14:27). God even counted the number of times they murmured against Him.

Amazingly, the Lord informed them one day that they had said those things on ten different occasions. God had secretly been recording their comments and complaints. God counts the number of times you complain and the things you say are also noted by angels.

> Because all those men which have seen my glory, and my miracles, which I did in Egypt and in the wilderness, and have tempted me now THESE TEN TIMES, and have not hearkened to my voice;
>
> Numbers 14:22

Perhaps you have wondered why there is no reaction from God when you murmur against His servants. The children of Israel had to murmur ten times before God reacted. They must have been shocked to find that God had been counting the number of times they had been speaking against Him.

Many sins are allowed to continue for years until the cup is full. When the cup is full, your sin will not be allowed to continue. You will bear the judgment for it.

Another reason why people murmur is because they are corrected, rebuked and warned about their bad behaviour. Many people react badly to correction and rebukes. They feel they are being badly treated. Instead of feeling that you are being maltreated, it is important that you see that God is correcting you for genuine errors you have made.

Anyone who is angry at authority is angry at God. It is your duty to flow with authorities that have been set by God.

> Let every soul be subject to the governing authorities. For there is no authority except from God, and the authorities that exist are appointed by God.
>
> Romans 13:1 (NKJV)

Decide that you will not be one of those who murmur against the leader. Murmuring is the distinctive sign of rebellion and disloyalty. I always watch out for people speaking undertone. I do not have to hear what they are saying. Once I notice people whispering; talking quietly but hushing up when I get near, I know that something is wrong.

Watch out for people who stop talking when you come into the room! Watch out for people who do not continue what they are saying when they see you. Watch out for people who cannot say to you what they were saying to others.

Watch out for people who seem to have something to say on the side whenever there is a meeting! Watch out for people who speak undertone to a neighbour whilst you are preaching. Watch out for all murmurers. Murmurers are dangerous people!

Murmuring will keep you from the call of God. Murmuring will keep you away from fulfilling your ministry. Murmuring reveals a bad attitude.

Murmuring reveals that you are not worthy of the high position that God is calling you to.

Murmuring reveals that you are in the wrong group. Murmuring reveals that you should find some other job to do, far away from the house of God.

Are you a murmurer? Do not complain about full-time ministry. Do not complain about your work. Do not complain about anything! Learn to work peacefully and have a good attitude.

Learn to have a pure heart! Learn to flow nicely and be cheerful about everything! Watch out for the sin of murmuring! Murmurers turn into gossips. Murmurers turn into bitter, malicious, damaging personalities. God is trying to save you from such wickedness. God is trying to help you to become one of the few that are chosen!

CHAPTER 27

Few Are Chosen because of Their Unbelief

Let us therefore fear, lest, a promise being left us of entering into his rest, any of you should seem to come short of it. For unto us was the gospel preached, as well as unto them: BUT THE WORD PREACHED DID NOT PROFIT THEM, NOT BEING MIXED WITH FAITH IN THEM THAT HEARD IT.

Hebrews 4:1-2

It is time to believe the call of God. God is sending you to the ends of the world. There is no need to complain. There is no need to doubt. Being in the ministry is all about walking by faith. You must believe in God and you must believe in His calling. Murmuring is a sign of unbelief. Unbelief is manifested in murmuring.

A manifestation of a lack of faith is a bad attitude. Watch out for those who have a positive attitude. Watch out for those who believe everything will be okay. Those are the people you need. Those are the people with the can-do spirit.

Do you want to be one of the few who are chosen? Then arise and shine! Do not look back! Do not doubt! Give up everything for the ministry. Throw yourself into His hands! Trust God to take care of you! When I came into the ministry, I did not know how I would survive. I did not know how I would have money to eat and to live. But God has taken care of me. He said to me, "Give yourself wholly to these things and your profiting will appear to all." I believed it and I gave myself wholly to the ministry. Indeed, my profiting has appeared.

When I look back at where we came from, I am amazed at what the Lord has done. I recently saw a video of the beginning of our church. What struck me was that I must have had great faith. Without faith, I would not have confidently led those young children from a corridor, to a canteen, to a cathedral. Without faith I would not have been happy to be serving the Lord. I have never been unhappy serving the Lord.

Every day in his service has been a day of joy, a day of adventure and a day of excitement.

One day I said to a friend, "Do not complain about the ministry. Do not say anything bad about the church. It is a good church. It is a blessing! We are blessed to be here."

One day, standing in a lift in Panama, I said to my pastor who was standing opposite me, "We are blessed!"

Then he replied, "It must be the many times you say 'We are blessed' that have brought such a blessing to us in the church." Instead of speaking your doubts and your fears, declare how blessed you are and how fortunate you are to be in His service. Over time, you will see that your faith has paid off.

Those who attempt to cross the Red Sea without faith cannot succeed at all. Those who have faith can cross the Red Sea to do exploits for God. Faith is your chance to subdue nations and win many battles for Jesus! Rise up, my friend and use faith to overcome in life and ministry and become one of the few who are chosen by God to serve Him.

You will soon be shining! You will soon be the talk of the town! You will soon be the city set on a hill that cannot be hid! You will soon be a light that is placed on top of a table! You will soon be the centre of attraction, just because you believed.

Remember that there is no good thing in you! There is no high level of morality that you can claim to have. All you can do is to believe in God and to trust Him every day of your life. Walk by faith and not by sight and you will experience great things in God. You will soon be declared one of the chosen few!

CHAPTER 28

Few Are Chosen because They Do Not Follow Fully

But my servant Caleb, because he had another spirit with him, and HATH FOLLOWED ME FULLY, him will I bring into the land whereinto he went; and his seed shall possess it.

Numbers 14:24

Over the years I can see how many are called but few are chosen because they do not follow *fully*. Many people claim to be followers. The main problem is that many people do not follow *fully*. Until you follow as though you are copying, you are not truly following *fully*.

Caleb and Joshua were different from all the others because they followed the Lord *fully*. It is easy to say you are a follower. Many who claim to be followers are really taking bits and pieces here and there and claiming to be followers when in actual fact they are very far from being true followers.

If you are following someone who is driving from New York to Florida, you are likely to see all the sights that he also sees. If you are following Jesus, you will see all the things that He saw on His journey to the cross and you will see all the characters that He saw on His journey to the cross. You will meet all the people He met. It is because you are following Him all the way!

Stop deceiving yourself that you are following when in actual fact you are not. I have been on a mission in Ghana for many years. God has used me to build churches and to conduct crusades. Those who are following me are equally building churches and conducting crusades.

Do you want to be successful in ministry? Learn the art of following *fully*! Allow yourself to stare at someone you claim you are following. Ask yourself the difference between yourself and that person. Try and find out some of the things that person does that you do not do. List them out and decide to do them. As you get closer, you will find many little things that are the reason for a person's success.

When Kenneth Hagin died, many ministers stepped out and gave testimonies about their experiences with Kenneth Hagin. One of them said, "When you experience Kenneth Hagin in a conference or in a church, you experience a man of faith."

Then he continued, "When you experience Kenneth Hagin at close range, you experience only love. There is hardly any faith. It is all about love."

Another said, "You will never hear him say anything bad about anyone. You never hear him making bad comments about people. Even when he was hurt by people he would always say, 'Just leave it to God.' Kenneth Hagin was full of love."

There are people who claim to be following Kenneth Hagin but do not realise that they are not following the love part of Hagin. Perhaps you just see him from afar and experience him as a man of faith. In order to follow him fully, you need to develop that kind of love people felt at close quarters.

Many are called but few are chosen because they do not follow fully! If you want to follow Kenneth Hagin, you have to follow his faith and also his love. Kenneth Hagin wrote a book titled, "Love, the way to victory"[1] You will never experience the victories that he experienced if you do not walk in love.

It is only when you look on with humility that God allows you to see and to notice things. After Kenneth Hagin died, I watched a video of his funeral several times. Each time I watched and heard the testimonies of those who knew him personally, I learnt something new.

I learnt things that I wanted to follow. I learnt about things that I needed to add to my life.

Become a humble servant of God with eyes of humility. Approach God's servants with humility and allow God to show you things that you can follow, so that one day it will be said of you that you have followed fully.

Not following fully is a cause of barrenness.

---

[1] Hagin, Kenneth E. *Love: The Way to Victory.* Faith Library Publications, 1994

People read books but are not able to achieve what the books teach. Then they say, "It does not work." But that is not true! If you follow fully you will see the same results! God is giving you a greater ministry. He is taking you out of the many who are called and bringing you to the few who are chosen. Become a man of faith and you will definitely be among the few who are chosen.

CHAPTER 29

Why Few Spies Are Chosen

And Moses sent them to spy out the land of Canaan, and said unto them, Get you up this way southward, and go up into the mountain: And see the land, what it is; and the people that dwelleth therein, whether they be strong or weak, few or many; And what the land is that they dwell in, whether it be good or bad; and what cities they be that they dwell in, whether in tents, or in strong holds; And what the land is, whether it be fat or lean, whether there be wood therein, or not. And be ye of good courage, and bring of the fruit of the land. Now the time was the time of the firstripe grapes.

So they went up, and searched the land from the wilderness of Zin unto Rehob, as men come to Hamath. And they ascended by the south, and came unto Hebron; where Ahiman, Sheshai, and Talmai, the children of Anak, were. (Now Hebron was built seven years before Zoan in Egypt.) And they came unto the brook of Eshcol, and cut down from thence a branch with one cluster of grapes, and they bare it between two upon a staff; and they brought of the pomegranates, and of the figs. The place was called the brook Eshcol, because of the cluster of grapes which the children of Israel cut down from thence.

Numbers 13:17-24

Twelve spies were sent out on a mission. They were asked to spy out the land and bring a report. Today, we know the names of only two of these spies. I dare you to mention the names of the other ten spies. No one knows their names because they are not worth remembering. What made Joshua and Caleb stand out among the twelve spies who were sent out on a mission? Why did God reject the ten spies and choose Joshua and Caleb to enter the Promised Land? Today, you have been sent on a mission just as the twelve spies were sent on a mission. Will you end up being one of the chosen spies?

Joshua started out as a spy. In the end he was chosen as the leader of the entire nation of Israel. God chose Joshua as a leader of the Israelites because he was faithful as a spy. Let us look at the reasons why twelve spies were sent out and only two were chosen.

1. Few spies were chosen because the others preferred to be among the majority and to please men.

Two spies were chosen because the other ten preferred to be among the majority. If you want to be among the majority, you will always lose your place with God. Accept to be one of the odd ones out. Do not worry if you are the odd one out. I have been the odd one out on many occasions. Even if you are the odd one out, once you have God on your side, you are in the majority.

And the Lord spake unto Moses, saying, Send thou men, that they may search the land of Canaan, which I give unto the children of Israel: of every tribe of their fathers shall ye send a man, every one a ruler among them. And Moses by the commandment of the Lord sent them from the wilderness of Paran: all those men were heads of the children of Israel.

Numbers 13:1-3

And they went and came to Moses, and to Aaron, and to all the congregation of the children of Israel, unto the wilderness of Paran, to Kadesh; and brought back word unto them, and unto all the congregation, and shewed them the fruit of the land. And they told him, and said, we came unto the land whither thou sentest us, and surely it floweth with milk and honey; and this is the fruit of it. Nevertheless the people be strong that dwell in the land, and the cities are walled, and very great: and moreover we saw the children of Anak there.

Numbers 13:26-28

2. Few spies were chosen because "many" called the Promised Land a bad land.

Only Joshua and Caleb called it a good land. You must believe that God has given you a good thing. God does not give you bad things. If you call the good thing that God has given you a bad thing, you must expect judgment.

Murmurers are wicked people. Murmurers pollute the minds of everyone. Murmurers turn the hearts and attitudes of people away from the leader. Murmurers make everything good look bad. Murmurers say bad things about all the nice things God has done for them. Those who speak in this way are always rejected.

And they brought up an evil report of the land which they had searched unto the children of Israel, saying, THE LAND, THROUGH WHICH WE HAVE GONE TO SEARCH IT, IS A LAND THAT EATETH UP THE INHABITANTS THEREOF; and all the people that we saw in it are men of a great stature. And there we saw the giants, the sons of Anak, which come of the giants: and we were in our own sight as grasshoppers, and so we were in their sight.

Numbers 13:32-33

3. **Few spies are chosen because "many" had a negative attitude. Few spies were chosen because "many" saw things in the wrong way.**

Seeing yourself as a grasshopper when God sees you as a conqueror is a sin. If you see love as lust, you are seeing things in the wrong way. Seeing a rebuke as hatred and maltreatment is seeing things in the wrong way. Seeing a correction as abuse and cruelty is an evil thing.

Always ask yourself what kind of attitude you have. Are you a positive person or a negative person? Decide to be one of the people who has a positive attitude towards the commands of God and the direction of the Holy Spirit. Many people are given to complaining.

And they told him, and said, we came unto the land whither thou sentest us, and surely it floweth with milk and honey; and this is the fruit of it. Nevertheless the people be strong that dwell in the land, and the cities are walled, and very great: and moreover we saw the children of Anak there. The Amalekites dwell in the land of the south: and the Hittites, and the Jebusites, and the Amorites, dwell in the mountains: and the Canaanites dwell by the sea, and by the coast of Jordan. And Caleb stilled the people before Moses, and said, Let us go up at once, and possess it; for we are well able to overcome it. But the men that went up with him said, we be not able to go up against the people; for they are stronger than we. AND THEY BROUGHT UP AN EVIL REPORT OF THE LAND WHICH THEY HAD SEARCHED UNTO THE CHILDREN OF ISRAEL, SAYING, THE LAND, THROUGH WHICH WE HAVE GONE TO SEARCH IT, IS A LAND THAT EATETH UP THE INHABITANTS THEREOF; AND ALL THE PEOPLE THAT WE SAW IN IT ARE MEN OF A GREAT STATURE.

Numbers 13:27-32

4. Few spies were chosen because "many" were afraid of giants.

There are giants today. The Promised Land was littered with giants. *Every Promised Land is littered with giants.* God is calling you to a land full of giants; financial giants, ministry giants, political giants, immigration giants, legal giants, medical giants – all kinds of giants. It is your duty to walk on fearlessly. Fear is a powerful weapon of the devil. When you overcome fear, you will overcome many enemies.

When you overcome fear, you are delivered out of the hand of your enemies. God is delivering you from the hands of the enemy so that you can serve Him without fear.

That he would grant unto us, that we being delivered out of the hand of our enemies might serve him without fear,

Luke 1:74

And they told him, and said, we came unto the land whither thou sentest us, and surely it floweth with milk and honey; and this is the fruit of it. NEVERTHELESS THE PEOPLE BE STRONG THAT DWELL IN THE LAND, AND THE CITIES ARE WALLED, AND VERY GREAT: AND MOREOVER WE SAW THE CHILDREN OF ANAK THERE. THE AMALEKITES DWELL IN THE LAND OF THE SOUTH: AND THE HITTITES, AND THE JEBUSITES, AND THE AMORITES, DWELL IN THE MOUNTAINS: AND THE CANAANITES DWELL BY THE SEA, AND BY THE COAST OF JORDAN. And Caleb stilled the people before Moses, and said, Let us go up at once, and possess it; for we are well able to overcome it. But the men that went up with him said, we be not able to go up against the people; for they are stronger than we. And they brought up an evil report of the land which they had searched unto the children of Israel, saying, The land, through which we have gone to search it, is a land that eateth up the inhabitants thereof; and all the people that we saw in it are men of a great stature.

Numbers 13:27-32

5.   **Few spies were chosen because "many" were rebellious and stirred up people to speak against Moses which is a sin.**

The other spies made the children of Israel turn against their leader. Anyone who makes you turn against your leader is an evil person. No matter who the person is, if he turns your heart against your leader, he is turning you against authority. Authorities are set there by God! Anything that turns your heart against authority is turning your heart against God. The ten spies caused the whole nation of Israel to be angry with Moses. Moses became unpopular because of the ten spies.

Moses was disliked because of the ten spies.

Moses was seen as an evil man because of the ten spies.

Moses was insulted because of the ten spies.

Moses was ashamed because of the ten spies.

Moses was almost killed because of the ten spies.

Moses was almost overthrown because of the ten spies.

Moses suffered great loss because of the ten spies.

These ten spies turned the hearts of the masses against their God-ordained leader. This wicked act of rebellion in spreading hatred toward leadership was judged by God. None of these ten spies entered the Promised Land. They were cast away in the wilderness and perished because of what they did against their leader (Numbers 14:36-37).

Watch out for anyone who poisons your heart against your leader. Watch out for anyone who whispers into your ear that your leader does not like you. Watch out for those who whisper among themselves and say, "He is just using you."

Watch out for those who whisper in your ears and say, "Is this all we get for all the hard work we have done?"

Be careful of every rebellious person, no matter the rank they are at! The devil himself comes in the cloak of an angel. Many angelic looking people are actually evil people. Watch out lest your heart is filled with rebellion! Today, God is setting you free from rebellious friends and rebellious leaders. You will be one of the few that will be chosen because you will escape a rebellious spirit and a rebellious attitude.

And all the congregation lifted up their voice, and cried; and the people wept that night. And all the children of Israel murmured against Moses and against Aaron: and the whole congregation said unto them, Would God that we had died in the land of Egypt! Or would God we had died in this wilderness! And wherefore hath the Lord brought us unto this land, to fall by the sword, that our wives and our children should be a prey? WERE IT NOT BETTER FOR US TO RETURN INTO EGYPT? AND THEY SAID ONE TO ANOTHER, LET US MAKE A CAPTAIN, AND LET US RETURN INTO EGYPT. Then Moses and Aaron fell on their faces before all the assembly of the congregation of the children of Israel.

Numbers 14:1-5

6.   **Few spies were chosen because they had a different spirit.**

But my servant Caleb, because HE HAD ANOTHER SPIRIT with him, and hath followed me fully, him will I bring into the land whereinto he went; and his seed shall possess it.

Numbers 14:24

Amazingly, it is the spirit that you carry that makes you follow someone. Having the right spirit is what will cause you to even be interested in being a hard follower and a true follower. There is a spirit called the spirit of disobedience. That spirit causes you to disobey in big things and also in little things. When you have the spirit of disobedience you constantly disobey instructions. You constantly resist instructions. You reject little commands and pieces of advice.

As you serve the Lord, you must ask yourself what kind of spirit you have. Evil spirits cannot express themselves because they are not human. They seek to sit on the shoulders of people and influence them to behave in a particular way. One of the amazing effects of an evil spirit is to make you unable to follow the person who God wants you to follow.

Many times, I have shared with people on how they can become great in the ministry. I would show many examples of how "following" has helped me to get very far in ministry. I would share how "following" has helped me to catch up and surge forward. Yet it seems that "following" is one of the most difficult things for people to do.

The spirit of a hard follower is the spirit that Joshua and Caleb had. The hard follower is actually the Spirit of humility. It is the Spirit of Christ. Jesus said, "I only do what I see my Father do. If I do not see my Father do it, I will not do it" (John 5:19). Without humility you can never be a hard follower. The keys and the answers will be staring at you. The revelation will be sitting right in front of you but you will be unable to follow it because the spirit within you is the spirit of disobedience.

No matter how clear and easy the instructions are, you simply want to do something different.

You simply want to introduce some variation!

You simply do not want to mention someone else's name!

You simply want to be at a place where you do not honour anyone!

Wherein in time past ye walked according to the course of this world, according to the prince of the power of the air, the spirit that now worketh in the children of disobedience:

Ephesians 2:2

Many are called but few are chosen! Few are chosen because they refuse to have the spirit of Joshua and Caleb who followed the Lord fully. You can follow God fully! You can follow God's servants fully! You can surge forward! You can catch up! You can become mighty in the spirit and mighty in ministry. Humble yourself and surge forward! Humble yourself and become all that God wants you to become!

Many are called but few are chosen! You will become one of the few that shine in the ministry. Beginning from now, your ministry will shine!

Your ministry will surge forward! Your ministry will become what God intends! Your ministry will become what God wants it to become! This is your time to follow fully!

CHAPTER 30

Why Few Survive the Wilderness of Ministry

For the Lord had said of them, They shall surely die in the wilderness. And there was not left a man of them, save Caleb the son of Jephunneh, and Joshua the son of Nun.

Numbers 26:65

Many of the Israelites launched out on the great adventure of following the Lord. Few of them actually made it to the end of the ministry. What happened in the wilderness is what will happen to you if you do not prepare and protect yourself. The wilderness of ministry is waiting for everyone who claims to be called by God. Most of the Israelites died in the wilderness. Most ministers perish in the wilderness of ministry and never make it to the heights they were originally called to.

1.   **Few survive in the wilderness because of the bitterness of life.**

> So Moses brought Israel from the Red sea, and they went out into the wilderness of Shur; and they went three days in the wilderness, and found no water. AND WHEN THEY CAME TO MARAH, THEY COULD NOT DRINK OF THE WATERS OF MARAH, FOR THEY WERE BITTER: therefore the name of it was called Marah. And the people murmured against Moses, saying, what shall we drink?
>
> Exodus 15:22-24

God will lead you to a bitter pool! It was not the devil who led them to the bitter pool! Indeed, there are many bitter experiences awaiting you in the ministry. When God led the children of Israel out of Egypt, He led them straight to the waters of Marah. The waters of Marah were bitter waters. God did not lead them to sweet waters. Do you think God does not know the way to sweet waters? God knows the way to every good place. But He led them to waters that were bitter. Marah was a great test to the children of Israel. Marah will be a test for you too!

Few are chosen because when they get to the bitter waters, their complaining, disloyal spirit is exposed. The fact that you cannot endure a little bitterness, a little sadness and a little disappointment reveals how shallow you are.

God has great things in store for you. You must accept the fact that on the journey to ministry, one of the very first stops is the bitter waters of Marah. It is at the bitter waters that a whole lot of people fall away. Do not fall away because of the bitterness that you experience in ministry. God loves you and He knows why He is bringing you to a place of bitterness.

I remember a man of God who experienced a great tragedy in his life. Years after this tragedy, he was called forward to come and celebrate and give thanks to the Lord. He said, "I will not celebrate and I will not rejoice in the Lord because God did not keep His covenant with me. I promised to serve the Lord and the Lord should have protected me from evil. Since the Lord did not keep His covenant, I do not see why I should rejoice in the Lord or celebrate."

Dear friends, do not allow the bitter waters that God has led you to, turn your heart against the Almighty God. Bitterness will be part of the high calling. If the Israelites were led straight to bitter waters, you can expect to experience the same thing.

You must survive this and go on, and you will become one of the few that are chosen.

2. Few survive in the ministry because their minds are on Egypt.

And they said unto Moses, BECAUSE THERE WERE NO GRAVES IN EGYPT, hast thou taken us away to die in the wilderness? wherefore hast thou dealt thus with us, to carry us forth out of Egypt?

Exodus 14:11

You cannot serve the Lord and have your mind elsewhere. As I travel around Africa having crusades, I have met many ministers whose minds are on politics.

There are many men of God who want to be presidents of their countries. I have also met ministers whose minds are on diamonds, gold and silver. Pastors desperately want to be business tycoons. Pastors want to own mines and rub shoulders with the top businessmen of our world. God has not called us to be businessmen. He has called us to be humble servants of God. He has called us to be priests who work in His house.

Be content with your call and you will be among the few that are chosen.

Many are called but few are chosen! Many are called but in the end only a few shine! Many are called but in the end only a few seem to excel in ministry. This is your day to shine! Keep your mind and your heart on God's calling. Do not try to be anything that God has not called you to be. How can you serve the Lord if your mind is on Egypt?

How can you follow Jesus and be a successful minister if your mind is on the world? Love not the world; neither the things that are in the world! (1 John 2:15). Anyone who loves the world does not love the Father!

3. Few survive in the wilderness because they follow the wrong leaders.

Now Korah, the son of Izhar, the son of Kohath, the son of Levi, and Dathan and Abiram, the sons of Eliab, and On, the son of Peleth, sons of Reuben, took men: And they rose up before Moses, with certain of the children of Israel, two hundred and fifty princes of the assembly, famous in the congregation, men of renown: And they gathered themselves together against Moses and against Aaron, and said unto them, Ye take too much upon you, seeing all the congregation are holy, every one of them, and the LORD is among them: wherefore then lift ye up yourselves above the congregation of the LORD?

Numbers 16:1-3

One of the reasons why people fall away in the wilderness is that they follow imposters. Korah rose up in rebellion in the wilderness. Korah became an alternative to Moses. Many people followed the rebellion of Korah. They were destroyed.

Make sure you are following the right leader. Do not allow satan to mislead you! Do not join any side group! Do not join an alternative leader! Do not let impressive, tall, nice-looking and holy-sounding men lead you astray! There are many men who look like angels. They appear holy! They appear righteous! They appear loyal! They appear wise, but in actual fact, they are carrying the spirit of Korah.

Hundreds of people perished in the rebellion of Korah. God always has a legitimate leader whom He has set up. Satan will always present a counterfeit. Satan is the master of counterfeit and falsehood. Satan is the master of disguise. He appears as an angel of light and many people think he is actually an angel. (2 Corinthians 11:13-15). It is time for you to humble yourself and follow the one whom God has ordained to be in charge. Do not follow the rebellion of Korah and you will be among the few that are chosen.

4. **Few survive in the wilderness because they do not learn how to overcome in conflicts.**

NOW THESE ARE THE NATIONS WHICH THE LORD LEFT, TO PROVE ISRAEL BY THEM, EVEN AS MANY OF ISRAEL AS HAD NOT KNOWN ALL THE WARS OF CANAAN; ONLY THAT THE GENERATIONS OF THE CHILDREN OF ISRAEL MIGHT KNOW, TO TEACH THEM WAR, AT THE LEAST SUCH AS BEFORE KNEW NOTHING THEREOF; Namely, five lords of the Philistines, and all the Canaanites, and the Sidonians, and the Hivites that dwelt in mount Lebanon, from mount Baalhermon unto the entering in of Hamath. And they were to prove Israel by them, to know whether they would hearken unto the commandments of the Lord which he commanded their fathers by the hand of Moses.

Judges 3:1-4

There are many conflicts in the wilderness. God left the Canaanites, the Philistines and the other nations in the wilderness so that the children of Israel would learn how to fight. God wanted to teach them the art of war. To be a good minister of Jesus Christ, you need to know how to fight. The whole of ministry is about fighting.

In my book, "A Good General" you will learn about fighting wars. When you are in the wilderness things are not easy. There is little water! There is little food! There is little relaxation! Through the hardships in the wilderness, you learn many things about God.

God wants you to fight and to win! God wants to raise up warriors! God wants battle-hardened soldiers to be in His army.

You must remember the great promise in the book of Revelation. The Lord Himself will lead us on a white horse against the armies of the wicked. One of the names of God is the Lord of Hosts. The Lord of Hosts is the same as the Lord of the Armies. Do you want to be in the army of the Lord? Do you want Jesus to lead you against the armies of the wicked one? God is raising you up to be one of the great solders and warriors. Do not allow yourself to be destroyed by the wars that God wants you to fight.

> And I saw heaven opened, and behold a white horse; and he that sat upon him was called Faithful and True, and in righteousness he doth judge and make war. His eyes were as a flame of fire, and on his head were many crowns; and he had a name written, that no man knew, but he himself. And he was clothed with a vesture dipped in blood: and his name is called The Word of God. And the armies which were in heaven followed him upon white horses, clothed in fine linen, white and clean. And out of his mouth goeth a sharp sword, that with it he should smite the nations: and he shall rule them with a rod of iron: and he treadeth the winepress of the fierceness and wrath of Almighty God.
>
> And he hath on his vesture and on his thigh a name written, KING OF KINGS, AND LORD OF LORDS.
>
> Revelation 19:11-16

5.   Few survive in the wilderness because they do not learn how to eat daily manna.

One of the most important things for ministry is to have a daily quiet time. God has a message for you every day. In the wilderness, the children of Israel were taught how to get daily manna. It was something they had to humble themselves to find. It was something they had to humble themselves to do. Amazingly, the Holy Spirit has something for you every day. You cannot rely on what He told you seven years ago. God is leading you every day and He is giving you a Word every day. Humble yourself and learn this amazing secret.

I once wrote a book about "The Quiet Time". Many people despised the book and thought it was a book for secondary school children. Many people would be surprised to find out that the quiet time is one of the greatest secrets for any minister.

Having my quiet time is one of my greatest secrets. A quiet time is a special time with God every day when He speaks to you and leads you. Almost all my messages come from the quiet times I have had with God.

It is during the quiet times that I receive my daily manna. God was trying to teach the children of Israel to depend on Him for a daily Word. This was one of the great lessons of the wilderness. Unfortunately, many ministers do not catch this revelation when they are in the wilderness. Instead of depending on the daily manna to take them out of the wilderness, they turn away from these basics and move into vain jangling.

And when the children of Israel saw it, they said one to another, IT IS MANNA: FOR THEY WIST NOT WHAT IT WAS. AND MOSES SAID UNTO THEM, THIS IS THE BREAD WHICH THE LORD HATH GIVEN YOU TO EAT. This is the thing which the Lord hath commanded, Gather of it every man according to his eating, an omer for every man, according to the number of your persons; take ye every man for them which are in his tents.

And the children of Israel did so, and gathered, some more, some less. And when they did mete it with an omer, he that gathered much had nothing over, and he that gathered little had no lack; they gathered every man according to his eating. And Moses said, Let no man leave of it till the morning. Notwithstanding they hearkened not unto Moses; but some of them left of it until the morning, and it bred worms, and stank: and Moses was wroth with them.

And they gathered it every morning, every man according to his eating: and when the sun waxed hot, it melted. And it came to pass, that on the sixth day they gathered twice as much bread, two omers for one man: and all the rulers of the congregation came and told Moses. And he said unto them, This is that which the Lord hath said, To morrow is the rest of the holy sabbath unto the Lord: bake that which ye will bake to day, and seethe that ye will seethe; and that which remaineth over lay up for you to be kept until the morning.

And they laid it up till the morning, as Moses bade: and it did not stink, neither was there any worm therein.

Exodus 16:15-24

Conclusion

Many are called but few are chosen!

My prayer is that you will be among the few that are chosen!

The Lord is lifting you up by the power and revelation you receive through this book.

To the making of many books there is no end!